CONCILIUM

Religion in the Seventies

CONCILIUM

THE CHURCHES
OF AFRICA:
FUTURE PROSPECTS

Edited by

Claude Geffré and
Bertrand Luneau

A CROSSROAD BOOK

The Seabury Press ● New York

1977
The Seabury Press
815 Second Avenue
New York, N.Y. 10017

Library of Congress Catalog Card Number:
ISBN: 0-8164-0364-3
ISBN: 0-8164-2150-1 (pbk.)

Printed in the United States of America

CONTENTS

Editorial   ix

The Churches in Africa between Past and Future
  SIDBE SEMPORÉ   1

A Changing Church in a Changing Continent
  MICHAEL SINGLETON   15

The African Christian in Search of Identity?
  F. EBOUSSI BOULAGA   26

The Demands of the Gospel and African Anthropology
  JACOB MEDÉWALÉ AGOSSOU   35

Ecclesial Ministry and the Problems of the Young
Churches
  JEAN-MARC ELA   45

Missionary Priests and the Future of the African
Churches
  EFOÉ JULIEN PÉNOUKOU   53

The Relations of the Local Churches with Rome and
the Function of the Episcopal Conference of Black
Africa
  JOACHIM N'DAYEN   60

The Prospects for the Faith among African Youth
  GÉRARD ESCHBACH   69

The New Gospel in a Millenarian Church
 ANSELME TITIANMA SANON   79

A Statistical Survey of Christians in Africa
 RENÉ LAURENTIN   94

Independent Churches of African Origin and Form
 HAROLD TURNER   105

The Chances of a Dialogue between Christianity and
Islam in Black Africa
 LUC MOREAU   112

Editorial

TO pose the question of the future of the black African churches may seem rather odd nowadays. One African in four is a Christian and the big wave is not finished yet. The great missionary effort of the last century produced a multitude of churches and Christian communities of all known denominations. The Catholic churches of Africa, with which this issue of *Concilium* is concerned, alone represent more than forty million faithful. These are churches which for the most part have their own African hierarchies and possess a moral authority which often exceeds the numerical importance of the community. It would be relatively simple and in certain respects permissible to say that the missionary era was successful: as in the parable of the sower, the grain has been multipled thirty, sixty, even a hundred times.

Yet the least informed observer feels a little uneasy. For it soon becomes clear that the great bulk of what was built at an enormous cost of men and money, has some pretty fragile foundations. Even though the African churches no longer have to fear the fate of Hippo and Carthage, which in their time were also flourishing churches, it is not certain that they will mature to the status of unique and irreplaceable members of the Church of Jesus Christ, thus fulfilling their basic vocation.

Semporé's article is an opportune reminder that the 'original sin' of a time when too often Christianization and colonization went hand in hand, has not really been forgiven, and will not be until the legitimate desire for roots and authenticity (which alone can give the African communities a unique profile) is satisfied.

The task is difficult, both because they have to find their way in a continent which is changing profoundly, and which has not yet reached lasting equilibrium (hence the uncertain relations between churches and political authorities examined by Singleton), and because today it is still necessary to define oneself by western norms whose claim to universality often seem derisory to Africans (see the contribution of Eboussi Boulaga).

However, these conflicts between the imperatives of 'Christian morality' and the customs sanctioned by venerable tradition are every-day affairs. It is no longer possible to adjourn this indispensable con-frontation between two ethics (one of which, from the start, has sup-pressed the other), by denying it any value; instead it seems that a better understanding of 'the African' and his world offers the chance of a surprising renewal (Agoussou).

However one approaches it, one thing is clear: the African churches have to be allowed to discover their future, to appoint the ministers they need, and to define with full responsibility the relations they wish to maintain with the mother churches, and with the first among them (Ela, Penoukou, Ndayen).

One worry remains in spite of everything, When this 'revolution' eventually occurs, it is not certain that the new generation will feel concerned. The problem of young people in the Christian communities is a first-rank one at present. Without falling into undue pessimism, we have to acknowledge the fact that the African churches, and above all those in charge of them, are sometimes at a loss what to do (Eschbach).

In the last analysis it will be necessary for the African churches originating in the West and bearing the lasting marks of that origin to agree to a new 'exodus'. Like Abraham leaving the ancestral ground and not knowing where he was going, they will have to abandon the safety of the existing wise orthodoxies, in order to reach a maturity which will be their own and now borrowed. Then they will testify anew to the originality of the Gospel. It should be clear to everyone that the old churches themselves are in need of this epiphany (Sanon).

This wager on the power of the Spirit is still worth making as long as the African churches do not surrender the responsibility for their future to anyone else.

Claude Geffré
R. B. Luneau

by the Vandals under Genseric and by the Muslim armies, is definitely of interest for anyone studying the situation of our churches today—for at a distance of fifteen centuries history seems to have repeated itself in the northern and southern Sahara.

The evangelization of northern Africa was, in fact, the result of Roman imperial colonization in Mediterranean Africa. The character of the north African churches was forged and developed according to the Roman model, the only one respected and used by Christian settlers in this part of the Empire. It is significant that at the end of the fourth century the then declining Roman Empire felt the need to coin the new term 'Romania' to characterize 'civilization' in the face of mounting 'barbarism'. By 'Romania' was meant the ensemble of cultural values and of Latin civilization, the intrinsic excellence and manifest superiority of which were worth preserving, defending and propagating against all odds. It was under the standard of 'Romania' that Jerome and others blindly destroyed the reputation of the "barbarian" peoples.[1]

The 'pieds-noirs' or European inhabitants of northern Africa— Augustine and the descendants of the Christian colonial settlers—had the task of establishing a Latin church which, in good faith, was to impose on the local population a Latin style of being Christian. The Latin church of Augustine, moreover, had simply inherited a state of affairs which could be traced back to the end of the second century and which made the Afro-Mediterranean church the cradle of Christian Latinity. A pioneer in the creation and use of Christian Latin, the north African Church was in the vanguard of the militants in the Latinisation of the customs and practices of western Christianity.[2] One became Latin in becoming Christian and, above all after the proclamation of Christianity as the state religion by Theodosius and Gratian, the Latinization extolled and practised throughout the Empire served as a guarantee of and support for Christianisation. The measures adopted at the centre of the Empire, which were aimed at achieving uniformity of language, law, religion, and even dress, were approved by Christians, who regarded them as aids to the rapid and smooth expansion of Christianity. Indeed, the highest church authorities recognized the colonial Roman Empire on the same grounds, as the declaration of Pope Leo I in the fifth century bears witness: 'It was specially suited to the divinely prepared work that many kingdoms should be united in a single empire, in order that one general, preached message might reach more rapidly all the peoples that the government of a single town groups together'.[3] The local cultures of the colonized peoples were consequently ignored, if not actually held in contempt. In north Africa the churches remained profoundly alien to the Berber world, to Kabylic culture[4] and the exclusive links they maintained with Roman culture prevented them from putting down deep roots among the non-Latin peoples. So much so, that they suffered the same fate as Rome and collapsed with the Empire. Northern Africa ceased at that moment to be Latin . . . and Christian.

The Recent and Ambiguous Past of the Church in Black Africa

Setting aside Ethiopia, where the Church can testify to a tradition of more than fifteen centuries,[5] one can say that the introduction of Christianity to Africa is a fairly recent phenomenon, the average age of the churches being about a hundred years.[6] Unfortunately, as earlier in northern Africa, the meeting of Africa and the Gospel has been fraught with ambiguities of the worst kind, and the echo of the hundred and one canon shots that announced the arrival of Christ in our continent can still be heard.

The heralds of the Gospel who disembarked in Africa had from the first a double handicap, inherited from the society and from the Church whose sons they were. In fact, the society to which they belonged was the same one that had plunged headlong into the colonial adventure. Whether he liked it or not, the missionary, from the very fact that he generally made his appearance alongside the soldier and the trader, had in part—without realizing or wishing it—distorted the very significance of his presence and his message. The concomitance of military missions, trading missions and religious missions resulted in many places in a real connivance. The similarity of the terminology adopted by each ('mission', 'station', 'post', 'branch establishment', and so on) could not but emphasize this tacit complicity which many, including the missionaries, have since denounced.

What is more, the missionary, a man of his time and his country of origin, was only too often a victim of the prejudices of that time and country. Now, the European countries had formed an image of the black man which could only vitiate relations between the two worlds. Indeed, since Luther's Commentary on Genesis 9 and 10, the Christian West had found the biblical basis it needed for justifying the slave trade, the colonial conquests and, today, apartheid: the blacks, it was argued, are the objects of a special curse of God, the curse pronounced against Cham, the son of Noah who was named 'father of the black races'.[7] Testifying to this belief, Père Libermann affirms, for example, that 'the blindess and the spirit of Satan are too deeply rooted in this people, and the curse of its father still rests on it; it will have to be redeemed by sufferings united to those of Jesus . . . in order to cancel the curse of God'.[8] A missionary bishop begged his correspondents to pray 'that the good God . . . may open at last to the pure light of faith the eyes of those unhappy children of Cham'.[9] The same request was to be addressed by a group of missionary bishops to the assembled fathers of the first Vatican Council. Africa is seen to bear on its brow the black star of Cham, which earns for those marked by it the label inferior race, oversize children, primitive and savage, animist, fetichist.

When he approached the African, the missionary had to struggle against the effects of this distorted gaze which his society of origin made him focus on the black man. In addition, his mission suffered from another handicap: that of the impoverishment of theology at the beginning of the twentieth century. The evangelization of Africa coincided with one of the worst periods for theology in the Catholic Church. In spite of Leo XIII's appeal for a renewal of Thomism, theology was stagnating in the waters of a decadent scholasticism. The missionary arriving in Africa was armed with a good will badly enlightened by an extremely deficient soteriology. Possessed of an absolute certainty that outside the Catholic Church no one could be saved, he regarded baptism as the saving rite which brought a man out of the state of certain damnation and introduced him into a state of virtual salvation. The 'pagan', on the other hand, was for the missionary, as for the Church as a whole, the idolator who was not only in error about God, but was a victim possessed by Satan, the inspirer of 'pagan' religions and institutions.

Unenlightened zeal can, however, bear fruit, so true is it that God writes straight with crooked lines. The compromises, the prejudices and the theological simplism have not prevented the missionaries from establishing the basis of what constitutes the Church of Christ in Africa today. The debit of the missionary period, which still weighs heavily on our fragile Church, is the shadow in a picture in which the light of the Gospel is shining brilliantly.

THE PRESENT

Liabilities

We are the heirs of this missionary church, built in haste for us and without us. Naturally there is no lack of liabilities to threaten the future: the unfamiliarity and inadequacy of the structures and methods handed down by the missionaries seriously hamper our progress; the severe dearth of leaders ordained for the essential ministries makes for an irresponsible Christianity, and plunges many communities into a serious state of emptiness and exhaustion; exaggerated dependence on the others for the supplying of our current needs in human and material resources is a source of depersonalisation for our churches; the sacraments continue to be 'administered' in a highly individualistic perspective, and too much emphasis on them leads to a devaluation and loss of the true meaning of sacrament, while at the same time giving our communities a deceptive aura of Christianity; sometimes a situation that is far too clerical and a pyramidal vision of the Church leave lay people no more than a small share in the conduct of their own affairs; pastoral activity, based on schemes envisaged for exclusively rural areas, is found to be ill-equipped, unsuitable and disorientated when it comes to confront the actual problems of galoping urbanization;[10] the instinct to conserve and preserve received formulae and institutions tends to favour the old and the *status quo,* disappointing the aspirations of young people attracted by the elements of change and renewal; very often, faith hardly dares to venture out of the arena of the sacred, and the silence in which we immure ourselves when confronted with the régimes and political struggles which determine the fate of Africans reveals in our Christianity a lack of the prophetic dimension;[11] finally, our attachment to Rome, a mixture of veneration and submission, sometimes seems to paralyse our initiative and damp our enthusiasm for the building of a truly African church.[12]

Advantages

All these weaknesses, which threaten to jeopardise our future, cannot, however, hide the real advantages we have at our disposal. There is, first of all, our youth—we have not yet got our own Christian traditions, the weight of which would predetermine our options; this is fortunate, and if it is true that we are far too caught up in the wrappings of the overseas and pre-Vatican II traditions which presided over the birth of our churches, we have at least the resources to free ourselves from them. Youth is a source of vitality, and one of the characteristics of our churches is the energy with which they try more or less successfully to incarnate the Gospel, and in spite of the poverty of our means and the handicaps of every kind that paralyse our efforts, the joy of living together as brothers and disciples characterizes our celebrations and proclaims the primacy of the forces of life. This optimistic energy rests on a traditional cultural substratum, the richness of which is still unexplored—the ever-present vitality of our cultures is something that should serve as a springboard and ally itself with the inherent dynamism of the Gospel. The political and social context in which we live constitutes, in addition, a powerful stimulus for our churches, which are ceaselessly called upon to make the newness of Jesus Christ significant for an Africa in travail, and the vastness and urgency of the task of building up every aspect of African man prevent the Church from lapsing into lethargy. If the progress made by Islam in certain parts of Africa seems extraordinary, that of the Church is not less remarkable, and the sympathy on which Christianity can count among many peoples should not be ignored. Finally, the simplicity and conviction with which a great number of Christians live is a sign of hope for the future.

The Missionaries

The 'missionary' period of our church is officially over. The African churches are no longer mere appendages of metropolitan churches, and 'Propaganda' is no longer minister for the colonies of the Vatican. All our churches have acquired their own personality, even if it is sometimes only at the purely juridical level. As paradox would have it, however, for the time being, and it may even be so for some time to come, the missionaries far outnumber their African colleagues.

Some of us—a tiny minority—adopt *vis-à-vis* the presence of white missionaries in Africa, the clearcut position of Eboussi, who calls for 'the orderly departure of missionaries from Africa'.[13] Others, following the Moratorium of CETA, invite the African churches 'to refuse to accept funds and personnel, this being the best way of giving the African church power to accomplish its mission in the African context'.[14] The African episcopate, however, has reacted vigourously against such approaches: 'We denounce as contrary to the Gospel any act or word, written or spoken, which could possibly impede co-operation between the old and the young churches'.[15] And again: 'The missionaries should take no account of these deceptive voices which claim that the time for missions is over or which consider missionaries should be treated as aliens'.[16]

The solution to the problem—for that is what it is—will come through the determination of our churches to act in such a way that we no longer need a massive missionary presence in order to survive. And because insufficient account has been taken of the daring recommendations and prophetic warnings of Piux XI, who in *Rerum ecclesiae* (1926) drew attention to the danger the perpetual importation of a clergy that is not 'chosen and drawn from the population' constitutes for our churches; because, after 50, 100 and 150 years of existence, most of our churches have not succeeded in producing trained personnel capable of making complete provision for the most elementary needs of the communities, we have no other option but to take up the challenge offered us by Paul VI when he called on us to be 'our own missionaries'. And that not so much by driving the missionaries out as by creating the conditions which will make them superfluous. That presupposes a clean break with a pastoral heritage that is frankly inadequate, and a profound reorganisation of structures and ministries. It is true that a large missionary presence in a given place can retard or obstruct the evolution of a church in certain sectors,[17] but we also find that their disappearance, whether progressive or brutal, from some countries, far from having opened the way to a far-sighted and radical revision of current ideas and practices, has rather served as a guarantee for a makeshift policy which absorbs the energies and saps the strength that remain in making the existing system work. The missionary question is thus the goad which forces the Church and the people to choose between a simple relief effort, impossible to carry out, and a radical recovery, which is both desirable and necessary.

The Urgent Need for Theological Work

Much will be said about theology in this issue. The urgent need for theological reflection and praxis is felt throughout the continent. We lack theologians and, in consequence, an appropriate theology. If we listened only to the most official pronouncements from the West,[18] we would end up prolonging indefinitely the state of dependence and theological emptiness in which we find ourselves.

We know well enough that alongside the western- and eastern-type theologies there is room for a southern type, of which the Latin American offers us an example in an as yet inchoate state, while Africa hesitates to declare itself.[19] Now, the present predicament of our countries constitutes in itself a theological focus of formidable significance. Never has a country seethed with so many simultaneous questions about man; about the purpose of life and the meaning of history; about the importance of cultures and the evolution of socio-political institutions; about the impact of the invisible and the role of intermediaries; about the usefulness of techniques and the necessity of God; about health and happiness, poverty and power, death and the after-life. In the face of all these problems, the churches are asked to make the Gospel credible to the eyes and heart of the African. They will scarcely be able to do so if they succumb to theological psittacosis, and go on repeating formulae elaborated or learned under other skies.

At the risk of provoking conflict, the southern theologies should translate the Gospel and the aspirations of the poor into a new language, a language which will make the cries of those who have no voice heard in a world that is ill-disposed to hear them. The north-south political dialogue is proving difficult, because those of the south cannot endure any longer a situation in which six per cent of the world population—the United States—consumes, by itself alone, forty per cent of the earth's resources. Theological dialogue between north and south may prove difficult, because those of the south can no longer accept that ninety-eight per cent of the power and production should be the preserve of the Latin and Anglo-Saxon North.

The hard realities of our world will see to it that our theology is marked by its own particular accents. Can it be that our history predisposes us to promote in the Church an openness and a flexibility that are the reverse of self-sufficiency and intolerance? A general attitude like this would lead African theology to opt for a theology of brotherhood, and to renounce the individualism of an antifraternal civilisation, which is translated, on the religious level, into impersonal dogmas, a competitive morality, and traditions unrelated to real life. Western 'Christian' civilization was born of theft—that of fire by Prometheus—and fratricide—the murder of Abel by his brother. This surrender of the world to blood and fire eventually alienated man and upset his relationship with God, with his fellow men and with the universe. In view of this, a theology of brotherhood should, on the one hand, reflect seriously on the implications of brotherhood as an evangelical goal, and, on the other, lead to action against anything which vitiates human relations. The promotion of the African and evangelical values of communion and solidarity in an enlarged brotherhood moves via the reconciling, healing experience of human relations.

The Sacraments

In the field of sacramental theology and practice our churches must make a great effort in order, on the one hand, to discover the profound meaning and purpose of the 'sacrament' in the African context, and, on the other, to give back life and substance to the different sacraments.

It is significant that terms such as 'baptism', 'eucharist', 'orders' and even 'sacrament' itself, have not been translated into a number of African languages. In my own language, a sacrament was defined as 'a medicine made up from words and things'. Which is precisely how the amulet or charm is defined. Nineteenth-century theology, as well as that of modern authors of manuals like Tanquerey or Noldin, tied us to a magical and mechanistic idea of sacrament and its effects. Even after Vatican II we remain marked by that decadent scholasticism which merely accentuated within us a centuries-old tendency. A reevaluation of the meaning and purpose of the sacrament in the African context is one of the primary tasks, theologically and pastorally speaking, of our churches. Without a re-definition that takes African sacramentalism into account, the Christian seven will become standardized as 'a medicine made up from words and things'.

Such an effort to re-evaluate will lead necessarily to a revision of pastoral practice where the sacraments are concerned. It is in sacramental practice, in fact, that our churches display most obviously the bonds of their dependence on foreigners; and it will be like this as long as we are obliged to fit ourselves into the rigid framework of the Latin rite.[20] The adaptations allowed us do not go far, and the results obtained sometimes border on the ridiculous. The introduction into a defined cultural framework of disparate elements taken out of their original cultural context has not had entirely happy results. The principle of the incarnation demands that we renounce our too facile rule of uniformity and transposition, in order that Christ might find on our soil and at the heart of our communities *all* the human means through which to signify and communicate his salvation.[21] The present situation is very embarrassing for our church, which is reduced to importing quantities of foreign materials for liturgical and sacramental celebrations: texts, vessels, vestments, oils, incense, bread, wine . . . and even 'Christian names'. I will spend a few moments here on one example, which is the test case: the eucharist.

The authenticity of the eucharist on African soil poses a particular and delicate problem, in so far as, a very literal interpretation of the 'species' used has prevailed for centuries in both East and West: bread made from wheat, wine from the vine. This interpretation belongs to ecclesiastical discipline, and not to dogma as such. And as classical a western theologian as Bouesse was not afraid, in 1951, to sustain the possibility of 'consecrating bread made from grains other than wheat in regions where wheat is not cultivated'.[22] The Church, it has been repeated since the time of Pius XII and John XXIII, is not bound to any one culture, and I would add: not even to the culture of wheat and wine. The presence at the heart of the Church of Asiatic and African peoples, for whom this culture is alien, should provoke a very legitimate and necessary diversification of ecclesiastical discipline. The increasingly widespread use of bread and wine in our countries is often invoked as an argument in favour of current ecclesiastical practice, but people forget to examine the true extent and the true *meaning* of this phenomenon. It is not a question of condemning the use of bread and wine in Africa, but of questioning their ability to signify the eucharist adequately for us. For most Africans these products are 'the white man's food'. They are fundamentally alien to our culture—bread and wine are *cultural* as well as nutritious entities—and they can symbolize, in spite of themselves, not only dependence on one culture, the Mediterranean; not only our tacit compromise with the 'privileged' minority in Africa who can use bread and wine as a regular thing; but also our alienation at the hands of a world which imposes its culture simultaneously with its products.[23]

In the last analysis, the case of the eucharist exposes the ambiguity inherent in a particular manifestation of Christianity, which on the one hand claims it is open to all men and all cultures, and on the other hesitates or refuses to incarnate itself in this man, this culture, the moment either steps outside a specific mode of existence. The seriousness with which the difficult question of the eucharist is tackled in Africa will allow one to hope for a better future where the other sacraments are concerned—notably Christian marriage, the history of which in the African context, is one of glaring failure.

Centrifugal Forces

One of the most characteristic aspects of Christianity in Africa is its tendency to fragment continually into a multiplicity of autonomous groups and denominations.[24] This centrifugal movement affects all the confessions and is a challenge to them all. A phenomenon so widespread cannot simply be explained in term of the hidden ambition of cunning exploiters of African credulity. Their existence, however ephemeral and anarchic, is an invitation to the original churches to recognize in themselves the inadequacies and the symptoms of sclerosis and exhaustion that provoke the fragmentation.

All the messianic, prophetic and healing churches, which grow up in Africa by the hundred, try in their own—totally African—way to answer the questions left unanswered by the traditional churches. The latter, of western confection, worked only what seemed to them the arable surface of the African people, leaving fallow a no man's land covered with clumps of questions, doubts, aspirations and feelings of dissatisfaction of every kind. Most independent African churches try to take up and integrate into the vision of faith they put forward this facet of the African personality which was ignored or overthrown by the traditional evangelization. The attempt to incarnate the faith at the heart of Africa relates to aspects of life so various as the concrete means of conciliating the invisible powere and protecting oneself against occult forces; the cult of ancestors and intermediaries; family structures and marriage customs; initiation; rites for the obtaining and fostering of health;[25] the community as the total milieu for life lived in solidarity with others;[26] the significance of the religious leader; miraculous interventions of God . . . and so on; in a word, all the passionate, problematic search for a flesh-and-blood happiness here and now, in the shade of the Ancestors and the light of the Gospel.

This quest for happiness resorts spontaneously to the essential elements of African religious language—which combines word, gesture and instrument and draws on biblical and traditional African symbols in order to express itself. Ancient gestures, like anointing, eating or washing, become fully human and sacramental as soon as, no longer stripped of their flesh in order to serve a dying cult, they are celebrated with the full impact of their natural dimensions.

Thus the separatist religious movements in Africa should be for the established churches, in their search for an authentically African and evangelical Christianity, a leavening as well as a source of irritation. Their reading of the Bible may sometimes be naive, but their reading of the realities of Africa deserves consideration and respect.

THE FUTURE

It is already with us in germ in the difficult, exhilarating present through which we are living, with its hopes and its anxieties. The conditions for a confident march into the future are in theory obvious: freedom of action, and sufficient trust on the part of the western churches; courage to make what breaks are necessary and to discover African ways of being Christian; a meeting in depth with the African, with his traditional and contemporary components; determination to bear witness, to the point of martyrdom, to the credibility of Jesus Christ and to the sacred value of human life.

The dangers which lie in wait for the African church are, above all, the cowardliness and fear which paralyze progress and effort. The courage to move into action is often wanting in many church authorities.

In short, the future of our churches will be a test of rejuvenation and authenticity. Born old about a hundred years ago, the African church resembles the Jesus of the Byzantine icons, whose child's body has the face of a grown man. Its face will only lose its lines in the fountain of youth which is the future, passage through which implies death to a past of borrowing and a responsibility. President Julius Nyerere of Tanzania has said that 'fear of the future has nothing to do with Christianity'. And Archbishop Tchidimbo of Conakry, writing in prison, concluded that: 'Christianity is above all a religion of the future. There lies the secret of its youth, its eternal youth'.

The Chinese have a proverb: 'When someone points a finger at the moon, the fool looks at the finger.' Let no one look at the finger that traced these lines, but at the horizons full of promise that he has done no more than indicate.

Translated by Sarah Fawcett

Notes

1. Five centuries previously, Cicero had however rejected the opposition Roman-barbarian, and to the ideal of *homo Romanus* had preferred the ideal of *homo humanus*. See J. Moltmann, *L'homme—Essai d'anthropologie chrétienne* (Paris, 1974), p. 19 (*Mensch-christliche Anthropologie in den Konflikten der Gegenwart*, Stuttgart, 1971).

2. It undoubtedly merits, from every point of view, the eulogy of the historian Prosper, who in the fifth century referred to its rôle in the Pelagian controversy: 'Africa, it is you who pursue with the greatest ardour the cause of our faith . . . What you decree is approved by Rome and followed by the Empire!' In A. Fliche and V. Martin, *Histoire de l'Eglise*, IV, p. 110.

3. Migne, *P.L.* LIV, p. 422.

4. Thus, for example, the adoption of Greek and then of Latin as liturgical languages appeared absolutely normal to the 'colonial' church, which resided in the midst of peoples who had their own languages. I do not know to what extent Augustine and his contemporaries made the effort to understand and use Punic in their catechesis (see on this point W. M. Green, 'Augustine's use of Punic' in *Semite and Oriental Studies* 11 (1951), pp. 179–90). I know for a fact that they never used it as a liturgical language.

5. It is symptomatic that the eastern type of Christianity which was developed and still exists in the Ethiopian churches did not spread into the rest of black Africa. Less apt than western Christianity to conquer and dominate, held in a state of vassalage by Egypt, and virtually without the psychological and material means necessary for its own expansion, Ethiopian Christianity preserved, whether by choice or resignation, the traditional African tolerance in religious matters, which does not encourage proselytism.

6. The abortive attempt to evangelize the Congolese areas during the fifteenth century was a fleeting interlude without a follow-up.

7. This popular belief is to be found even in the *Petit Larousse*, and the latest of the great French translations of the Bible, the *Traduction Oecumenique de la Bible*, was forced to react explicitly against an "exegesis" that is still current in some churches, notably in South Africa. See T.O.B. (Paris, 1975) Gen 9:26, note f.

8. In G. Goyau, *La France Missionnaire dans les 5 parties du monde* (Paris, 1948), II, p. 117.

9. Mgr Augouard, *Vingt-huit années au Congo,* cited in 'Les plus beaux textes sur les missions', p. 311.

10. Africa is at present the least urbanized continent of the globe, but also the one with the highest rate of urbanization. Kinshasa, Zaire, for example, with an annual urbanization rate of twelve per cent, could double its population in six years.

11. Faced with situations like that in southern Africa, with the manoeuvres of the powers and super-powers, with the activities and counter-activities of the capitalist, socialist-Marxist or *sui generis* régimes that govern us, it would seem that the Gospel had taught us to keep our mouths shut. A certain fear of

politics could well explain this abstentionist attitude which, for many crushed, humiliated people, is no bearer of good news.

12. It seems that we have difficulty in combining communion with Rome with obedience to the Spirit, the source of life and energy. If the continuance, via the person of the pope, of our traditional veneration of the chief is something legitimate, the same cannot be said of the blocks he sometimes creates at the level of reflection and pastoral action. Communion with Peter should never be allowed to become that petrifaction of the spirit which is the cause of so much conformism and so many inhibitions.

13. F. B. Eboussi, 'La démission', *Spiritus* 56 (May–August 1974), pp. 276–87.

14. This 'moratorium' was adopted officially in May 1974 by CETA (Conference des Eglises de Toute l'Afrique) which numbers about a hundred member churches.

15. Declaration of the African bishops who attended the Roman Synod of 1974.

16. Declaration of the bishops of eastern Africa, cited in *Telema* 2 (July, 1975), p. 77.

17. Regarding the reconversion of the missionaries, I have always hoped that an organization or institute might be founded which would send out across Europe and America an army of missionaries of a new type, desirous of consecrating their lives to combating the structures (mental, political and economic) which allowed their countries to exploit us. I am willing to bet that such a mission would win the support of Africa and the 'southern world' as a whole.

18. One of the most recent came from Mgr Giovanni Benelli, Substitute Secretary of State, who said in February 1976 at Abidjan: 'There is only one universal theology, just as there is only one faith, one unique message of Christ, one single Catholic Church.' It is arguable that few theologians subscribe to this opinion which, in order to reject the pluralism—*de jure* and *de facto*—of the Christian interpretations of Christ's message, bases its arguments on the unity of the Faith, of the message and of the Church. I am very much afraid that very different realities are indicated by the word 'theology'. Ever since the New Testament itself accustomed us to a plurality of understandings and interpretations of the unique message of Christ, the perspective of a 'universal theology' seems relagated to the eschatological horizon.

19. This is due to the fact that we have lost a certain amount of time asking ourselves whether an 'African theology' is legitimate. In addition to the annual Theological Weeks at Kinshasa (Zaïre), the theological meetings at Jos in Nigeria (September, 1975) and at Dar-es-Salaam in Tanzania (August 1976) will, one hopes, help to clear away the block in Africa and stimulate research.

20. It has been said of the linguist Roman Jakobson that he spoke Russian fluently in six languages. Obliged to pour all the expressions of its liturgical vitality into the Latin mould, our African church contrives to speak Latin in hundreds of languages. The church authorities are increasingly coming to recognize the need for ritual changes in Africa, as this recent declaration of one of their number bears witness: 'The Roman rite that we follow was not chosen by us, it was imposed on us and it bears the strong imprint of western culture.

Since the council recognized the dignity and the particular personality of the local churches, rather than a reformed rite that leaves us ill at ease, should not the individual churches be allowed to elaborate their own rite, more suited to the genius and culture of their peoples?' (Mgr C. Guirma in *Le Calao*, 35 (1976-3), p. 33).

21. Liturgical pluralism must be extended to Africa itself, since it is not easy to see a single rite being established—which one?—which could claim to do justice to African sensibilities. Thus different African rites should develop, of which the liturgical experiments carried out at Kinshasa and Yaoundé are but a pale outline. The Catholic Church in Egypt provides a good example of such diversity, for the Latin, Maronite, Coptic, Greek, Armenian, Syrian and Chaldean rites, all of them Catholic, exist side by side on the same ground.

22. H. Bouesse, *Le Sauveur du Monde*, IV, 'L'Economie sacramentaire', pp. 59–68. R. Luneau has also touched on this question in 'Une Eucharistie sans pain et vin?', *Spiritus* 48 (1972), pp. 3–11.

23. Bread and wine are by no means neutral symbols in Africa: they 'classify' those who make them the basis of their daily diet, and their fundamental foreignness is made apparent by the fact that they are not normally translated in the texts of the canon of the mass.

24. D. D. Barrett, in *Schism and Renewal in Modern Africa* (Oxford, 1968), lists as many as six thousand separatist religious movements and groupings in Africa. If his conclusions about the causes of religious separatism in Africa are interesting, his methods of analysis and his classifications are, on the contrary, open to question.

25. The original, etymological connection between health and salvation is reaffirmed and underlined in the doctrine and in the cultic celebrations of many of these African churches.

26. African communitarianism, neglected and partially destroyed by western individualism, is here reinstated, and some churches try to recreate Christian *Umma* within which their adherents rediscover the security of finding all aspects of their lives taken effectively into account.

Michael Singleton

A Changing Church in a Changing Continent

HARDLY a decade ago, the data discussed here would have been automatically headed 'Church and State in Africa'. The discussion itself would have turned around the *de facto* tensions which arise between ecclesiastics and politicians—tensions for which the social encyclicals,[1] given their distinction between the things of God and Caesar's, could see no theoretical justification. Today, however, as Bishop Sangu remarked in Rome, September 1975, to the fourth plenary assembly of SECAM (the Symposium of Episcopal Conferences of Africa and Madagascar) 'the old theory of the Church and the State as two perfect societies, is clearly out-dated' even though 'no clear theory to replace it has, as yet emerged.' A mere description, then, of recent Church-State relationships in Africa would beg more questions than it solved. We have consequently chosen to examine some of the factors involved in the Roman Catholic Church's[2] search for a fresh identity and new role in the setting of Africa's increasingly authoritarian and socialist régimes.

THE ECONOMICS AND ECUMENICS OF CATHOLIC CHANGE

Though the epithet 'Roman' will have irritated some Catholics, it does pinpoint this particular Church's predicament in Africa. The Latinity of the Catholic Church amongst the Ibo, struck a recent theological tourist of note (A. Hanson, *The Times*, 5.6.1976). The Roman features of the Catholic Church in Africa are sometimes attributed to its financial dependence on the Vatican. But would funds from alternative sources be automatically applied to aims more African than those apparently paramount in many ecclesiastical circles? African bishops seem bent on possessing the full panoply of their western counterparts. But are major seminaries and congregations of sisters any more indispensable to Third World dioceses than national airlines and prestigious presidential palaces are absolutely necessary for developing countries?

Considerations such as these coupled with the self-reliant examples of independent churches have convinced some Africans that a moratorium on external financing as well as on expatriate personnel would oblige the mainline denominations to adopt a more convincingly African physiognomy. These are minority voices, however. The majority want Western money and to dispose of it according to their own priorities.[3]

If increased economic independence would not *ipso facto* solve the Catholic Church's African identity crisis, would an ecumenical adaptation to the African religious scene, be it Christian or traditional, prove more effective?

While the Africanness of the independent churches is as uncontrived as it is incontrovertible, it is not without certain ambiguities. The fact, for instance, that the Kimbanguist church uses African elements in the eucharist and does not use water in baptism indicates a potentially deeper understanding of sacramentality than that tolerated by the thresholds of reform fixed by Rome. The fact, however, that the Kimbanguists dissociated themselves from fellow patriots who protested against the colonial régime, is an option which would appear suspect in the eyes of theologians, black or otherwise, for whom freedom fighting and the Gospel are more than compatible.

By being too 'particular' a Church can compromise its credibility as the reincarnation of a Christ, who, if Küng, let alone Belo, is right, was anything but a soothing sacralizer of the *status quo*. Many of the new religious movements in Africa seem as likely to contribute realistically to nation building as were earlier Christians able to rapidly improve on the lot of women or slaves.

The diffidence manifested by most African politicians towards indigenous religious movements, even those of Christian inspiration, is perhaps motivated by their seeming incapacity to tackle problems at levels where effective solutions usually emerge. While some leaders dallied with these movements, none ever went so far as to establish them as national churches. Henry VIII might have been an Anglican but Mobutu is no Kimbanguist. What tendency there is, for instance, in Ethiopia and Mozambique, is towards the disestablishment of churches established by tradition or colonial power, and the suppression of sects which detract from national unity.[4] Any unreflecting alignment of the

Catholic Church with these African churches or indiscriminate assimilation of their salient features would not only alienate ordinary (Roman) Catholics but peripheralize even further this particular Church's participation in the determining of national destinies.

Changing Catholic Christianity in a wider ecumenical direction would seem even more equivocal. It is not that all African religions are doomed to die; some, indeed, have shown a remarkable degree of self-reliance and adaptive resilience. It is rather that an identity-seeking dialogue with traditional religions, even where it is possible, can divert attention from issues which might prove far more fundamental. All too often, moreover, this dialogue, though undertaken with the best of intentions, degenerates into a cannibalizing monologue. Not only is violence done to ethnographic facts, as when a longing for individual immortality is read into ancestor worship, but primitive culture is pillaged for elements that can be incorporated into the classically conceived sacerdotal and sacramental structure of the Catholic Church. But is the role of religious ritual so self-evident, will the eternal place of the priesthood, of which the psalmist speaks, always have an earthly echo? Can one conclude to dialogue with primitive religion before these more basic premisses have been established?

Islam in the short run and, more definitively, the secular(izing) State are likely to prove far more decisive interlocutors for the future of Catholic Christianity in Africa than either traditional religionists or other Christians.

THE CHURCH AND POLITICAL CHANGE

Of the 47 members present at the thirteenth summit conference of the Organization of African Unity held in July 1976 exactly 25 years after Libya had started the continent's move towards independent nationhood, 23 had undergone military coups and half of these more than once. However, as *The Economist* pointed out (13.3.1976, p. 58), this volatility was less impressive than Latin America's and masked the emergence of a broad African pattern. There is scarcely a country on the continent which has not shed the political structures bequeathed to it by the departing colonial powers and adopted at least the appearances of a radically rural and revolutionary socialism.

This move towards totalitarian regimes, be they one party—29 of the 32 countries with civilian governments are thus ruled—or military, has been contradictorily evaluated. On the one hand are those convinced that 'there is only one kind of political freedom' which, while it might 'not exist perfectly in the United States, or anywhere else for that matter,' does exist there 'and in some 27 other countries of the world, and does not exist anywhere else.'[5] The apologists of African socialism, on the other hand, retort that a westernised élite's forfeiting its freedom to exploit and egoistically enjoy, has been amply compensated by an immense improvement in the people's material decencies and national dignity.

At its November 1974 meeting in Accra, SECAM's Committee for African Internal Affairs (CAIA) steered a middle course between these two extremes. While expressing concern over 'the gradual monopolization of power by one man or party' with its subsequent 'suppression of all opposition', the bishops stopped short of outrightly condemning this continent-wide trend on the grounds of some absolutely objective, univocal understanding of liberty. The CAIA appears to allow for the finding of a freedom beyond the practice of both western-style liberal democracies and authoritarian African Socialism.

Merely tolerating the suspension of civil liberties until such a time as political maturity and social well-being were minimally achieved would surely not represent a creative contribution to the quest for an African understanding of freedom. Concretely, African Catholics are called upon to hammer out an adequate but adapted notion of human rights in two types of political contexts, the one neutrally if not positively disposed towards religion, the other indifferent and at times hostile. Tanzania and Mozambique will be taken as illustrative of these types.

TANZANIA: AN EXCEPTIONAL CASE IN MORE SENSE THAN ONE?

It would be difficult to discover a country more benignly disposed towards Christianity than Nyerere's Tanzania. Why then, wonder more leftward-leaning commentators, has the Catholic Church not seized the opportunity to divest itself of Western superstructures and reassemble itself along more socialist lines? The reasons for this reticence are as complex in their latency as they are ambivalent in their patency.

In the first place, Tanzanian churchmen appear intuitively more aware than those who have attempted it, of the far reaching repercussions any thorough going integration with the socialist system would have. Rome saw clearly—which is not to say correctly—that the worker priest experiment implied no mere reform but a radical transformation of the traditional priesthood. The Tanzanian bishops rightly fear that a certain kind of church—the one to which they are most attached—would disappear were there a massive migration of missionaries, let alone local clergy, to the *ujamaa* villages.[6]

In the second place, the gap between top and bottom can be as great in a one-party state as in a monarchically-organized Church. When he separates the spheres of religion and politics, Nyerere is speaking a sectorial language the bishops can understand. It is useful to reassure people trained to see in socialism a front for atheistic materialism that *ujamaa* contains nothing against faith or morals. In this author's own experience, however, these presidential distinctions can be interpreted lower down the line as a license to privatize and peripheralize religion out of all social relevance. While the uncooperativeness and at times open hostility of local officials in no way detracts from the sincerity of top level declarations, their existence partly accounts for ecclesiastics wanting to look before leaping onto the socialist bandwagon.

If it is utopian to expect the present hierarchies in socialist countries such as Tanzania to willingly dismantle the only church they have known, there is on the contrary, a prophetical rôle they could more energetically assume since many an African president has invited them to do so.[7] Paradoxically, there are perhaps as many strictly political as purely evangelical reasons for churchmen raising their prophetical voices more loudly in one-party states.

There are the poor to be protected. A Church worthy of Christ's name will at least act as watchdog for the underdog. The poor, however, in one-party states are likely to be deposed chiefs, disgruntled elders, alienated élites and scapegoat minorities. Is it not in the very interests of the party to promote a safety-valve institution such as the Church, which can prevent over heating of the system or even withdrawal from it? Could the Church not bring back the energy and expertise of such groups for the good of the country as a whole?

In fact, though there are noticeable exceptions to it and sociological explanations for it,[8] the tendency has been for this prophetical voice to be raised at once selectively and negatively. Scarcely audible in the presence of criminal abuse or unjust structures—the massacres in Burundi or the corruptions of Kenya's ruling clique—hierarchical noise becomes positively deafening when sexual matters are at stake. Whereas papal pronouncements on social issues are hardly echoed, Vatican documents on sexual mores meet with choruses of episcopal approval.

For the time being, the Tanzanian type of situation might not clearly call for some radical change in the Church. Some change, however, in the direction of a more operative if critical solidarity with African socialism is surely called for, otherwise the Church will find itself as emasculated and marginalized as it has become in other countries where it failed to react with sufficient radicalness to the signs of dawning times.

MOZAMBIQUE: AN EXCEPTION WHICH MIGHT PROVE THE RULE?

For all its desirability, one wonders whether the Church would be well advised to take the Tanzanian case as truly typical? Is not

conflict—not necessarily violent—the normal condition, both historically and ideally, of Church-State relationships? By considering
Mozambique as a pattern setting pacemaker for the continent as a
whole, the minimal conditions for ecclesial existence could perhaps be
more prudently envisaged in advance than the maximal ones con-
templated by a Barrett or Bühlmann.[9]

Of countries such as Equatorial Guinea, where the Church is subject
to a viciously vindictive persecution, there is little an outsider can say,
except that ideally martyrs should witness to fundamental Christian
values rather than stand on superficial, clerical privileges. It would be
odious for an outsider to say who had and who had not died for a good
cause. When the involvement of significant sections of the clergy in the
defence of European minorities is at least tolerated, why should similar
preoccupations on the part of African priests be castigated as tribalism,
especially there where the struggle is neither for regional egoism nor for
élitist privileges?

Nor is it easy for an outsider to judge matters which divide insiders
amongst themselves. The clergy of Togo and Zaïre, for example, appear as divided about the significance of Africanizing baptismal names
as was the French clergy over the meaning of revolutionary changes in
the calendar's nomenclature. However, while there is often more than
meets the eye in seemingly trivial innovations, seen from the side of the
people, is there finally more at stake than a power struggle or demarca-
tion dispute between priests and politicians?

Of countries with highly unpredictable leadership such as Uganda or
an extremely labile, love-hate relationship such as Zaïre, little definite
can be said either. Such cases do illustrate, however, the extent to
which relations between church and state in Africa often depend more
on personalities than principles. Whereas in Tanzania the Church's
schools were handed over to the government and the party's youth
league welcomed into the seminaries, the handling of both issues
proved traumatic to all concerned in Zaïre.

As for African countries with as liberal an economy as Kenya,
Nigeria or the Ivory Coast, competent commentators have wondered
how long it will be before the polarization characteristic of their Latin
American counterparts, will break out within both Church and State.[10]
Mozambique, on the other hand, given its Far Eastern[11] as well as its
African parallels, furnishes in all probability the ideal-type of testing
ground for the sincerity of the Catholic Church's recently declared
intentions of taking small-scale Christian communities seriously. It is
indeed in this direction that the Church has been contemplating the
kind of change which would furnish it with that new identity it so
ardently seeks.

Uncontroverted information[12] about the religious situation in

Mozambique is not easy to come by. Public measures such as the nationalization of schools, the freezing of Church funds, the closing of minor seminaries, the curtailing of missionary presence, would seem indicative of attempts to de-institutionalize Catholic Christianity. The atheism of the media coupled with the anti-religious aims of more confidential documents appear to reflect at least an élite's desire to subjectivise faith into redundancy. Mozambique's Chinese-style socialism, moreover, leaves little room for sacred specialists of any sort, pagan let alone Christian. The worker-priest ideal has become the norm for all and not just a few eccentric clerics.

The fact that Christians as a whole have sincerely beaten their breasts over compromises with colonialism, let alone that some paid the price for protesting against imperial oppression, is not sufficient in the opinion of régimes as radical as Mozambique's, to warrant the Church's continuing a chastened but conventionally conceived existence. Small wonder then, that 'the systematic formation of small Christian communities' which elsewhere in Africa is considered to be 'the key pastoral priority in the years to come',[13] constitutes in the episcopal eyes of Mozambique, an immediate *sine qua non* for Christianity's very survival.

The pronouncements of the Mozambique bishops are at once noticeably more urgent and remarkably less *dirigiste* than those of their colleagues elsewhere on the Continent. 'The time of prescriptions has passed. Concrete solutions will have to come from the whole people of God . . . A Church which is not of the people, nor animated by walking with the people, will have no place in the history which independent Mozambique has initiated. This also means that pastoral activities must come out of the communities and not from the missionary or a missionary team isolated at the top of the pyramid . . . the initiatives and objectives must come out of the communities and must be assumed by them.'[14]

The shape of a local church obliged by circumstances to shift its centre of gravity to small-scale communities, will be significantly other than that of a local church proposing to impose such structures as a solution to its pastoral problems. The latter, having initiated the discourse about small communities, will tend to lay down a priori the limits to which people can participate in the Church's mission—still substantially conceived on clerical lines. 'No action is to be undertaken without the consent of the bishop' said a speaker at SECAM's 1975 meeting. Like St Paul, those doing most of the talking and writing about local churches rarely live in one themselves.

Unlike St Paul, however, today's ecclesiastical authorities seem determined to keep a controlling interest over grass root groups. Though they will allow communities to participate in their apostolate just as they once allowed the catechist, there is no question of their being accountable to the people. If one allowed local communities to determine by deliberative procedures the type of ministers and ministry they wanted, would one not end up much sooner than later with married and even women priests? Unless circumstances decide otherwise, there are few bishops who believe God wanted them to be accountable so decisively to the inspirations of local congregations.

In Algeria, however, as in Mozambique, circumstances do seem to have persuaded some bishops that the physiognomy of basic Christian communities is to be invented heuristically rather than imposed hierarchically.

Reflecting on the experience of a Christian minority seeking its identity in face of an increasingly monolithic Muslim majority, Mgr Teissier, Bishop of Oran (Algeria), drew these tentative ecclesiological conclusions: 1. a growing awareness that the Church was not constituted once and for all with self-explanatory aims and one set of structures to implement them. On the contrary, the Church continually takes cues as to its identity from a genuine dialogue with other cultures; 2. a sinking suspicion that basic Christian communities should not be considered as the seeds or cells of a more fully fledged Church but are local[15] churches in their own right, anticipations, perhaps, of the only type the contingencies of tomorrow's world will allow; 3. a gradual realization of the ambiguity in assuming that the Church's being stripped of its schools, hospitals or development projects, means that its sacramental and spiritual rôle can shine forth more purely than ever before.

This third intimation is of especial importance to the last of the large Churches to be brought by historical circumstances to seriously envisage the need for a radical declergification. Up till now, when governments have taken over the Church's educational and medical institutions, the clergy have usually minimized the significance of this evolution by implying that these were, after all, only indirect means of apostolate. But besides inferiorising the activities of sisters, brothers and lay people, did not this dichotomy gratuitously equate the Church's essence with the direct, priestly apostolate?

Mgr Teissier wonders whether we should continue to identify even the priestly life with the sacramental animation of a Christian community.[16] The future surely reserves little room for that type of priest who withdrew into the Holy of Holies, there to perform sacred mysteries on the people's behalf. Will there, in the long run, be much more room for that type of priest whose permanent profession is to cater for the broadly spiritual as well as strictly sacramental needs of a Church, which to all intents and purposes, will be co-terminus with small scale Christian communities? There will, on the other hand, always be need for someone to build Christian bridges over the gaps between groups and cultures. There will always be room, as Teilhard de Chardin would have put it, for an activator of specifically Christian energy.

FROM A 'CHANGING CHURCH' TO 'CHANGING A CHURCH'

During the colonial period, the change with which the Catholic Church in Africa was most concerned was its own change from an embryonic to a fully-equipped branch of the Roman communion. It not only knew what was needed for canonical maturity but felt confident it would sooner or later obtain it. This confidence the Church had in its ability to change itself has given way of late to confusion as changes are forced upon the Church by circumstances beyond its control.

The one problem now is how can the Church get a grip on itself again? It is only when it will be in charge of it's own change that it can relate Christ convincingly to the changing continent. To do this, it must make up it's mind about basic Christian communities. Are the extra-sacramental, extra-sacerdotal communities which changes in the continent are likely to impose on the Church, simply temporary shelters in which Christians will have to weather out the coming secularist storm, before being able to build the Church back to its proper size, or are they already the shape of better things to come?

Though it would be in the interests of one-party states to have the Church massively there where it could be neutralized, would not the interests of Christ be better served by having Christians congregate in communities so subtly structured as to be difficult to detect let alone dismantle? Governments can close churches and ban priests as well as confiscate schools or hospitals. But there is one thing any system no matter how hostile would have difficulty in suppressing: the Christian fellowship of an informally organized community.

When the downhearted disciples recognized the risen Christ at Emmaus it was not because their Master had started saying mass but simply because he'd shared their meal. To change the Catholic Church in this direction might not be for the better but it would surely not be for the worse.

Notes

1. The Anglican bishop of Maseno, Kenya, echoes the classical Catholic teaching when he claims that 'these two institutions—Church and state—are divinely and independently appointed by God.' H. Okullu, *Church and Politics in East Africa* (Nairobi, 1974) (excerpted in *Uhuru and Harambee: Kenya in search of Freedom and Unity*, IDOC dossier 14, Rome 1975, p. 72). While one hesitates to call God's what in this case is clearly Constantine's, Bishop Okullu

is among the few African theologians who have reflected on their faith's relations to politics.

2. If throughout this article 'Church' is frequently shorthand for the 'Roman
Catholic Church' and this latter for the 'Roman Catholic hierarchy' it is because this Church's predicament in Africa acutely illustrates that of its
sociological similars and because this Church's position is principally known
through episcopal pronouncements. Thus it is change as it affects the ecclesiastical establishment which is envisaged here—the Christian people are wont to
pull through with or without the clergy.

3. Though often manifestly purely pastoral, the projects of Third World
ecclesiastics are nearly always latently socio-economic. P. K. Sarpong, Bishop
of Kumasi, Ghana, has tellingly pointed out that though his people will tolerate
only a one purpose church, the building functions in fact multi-purposely,
'Should we build Churches or Social Centres?', Worldmission, 26, 2 (1975), pp.
14–17.

4. While the Watchtower is not easy to accommodate in any modern state, it
is a pity its suppression in Malawi, Zambia and Mozambique should be so
patently linked to the consolidation of 'one-party dictatorial régimes'. T.
Hodges, 'Jehovah's Witnesses in Central Africa', Minority Rights Group, Report 29 (London, 1976).

5. A. M. Greeley, 'American Catholicism: 200 Years and Counting', The
Critic, 34, 4 (1976), p. 22. However, as the Third World theologians who met in
Dar-es-Salaam, August 1976, also protested about the lack of freedom in some
countries, it would clearly be out of place for an outsider to white-wash each
and every form of African Socialism.

6. Much has been written about Mgr Mwoleka, the ujamaa bishop—perhaps
too much, for he is as untypical of Africa as Helder Camara is of Latin
America—and he has explained himself on more than one occasion, cf. his
introduction to the roneotyped report of expatriate experiences in ujamaa villages: 'New Ways of Sharing in Community,' Rulenge diocese, Tanzania, 1975;
cf. also: Sr M. Salat, 'Living in Ujamaa Villages—a Reflection,' SEDOS,
Rome, 1976, pp. 197–99; M. Singleton, 'Prêtre ouvrier-prêtre ujamaa?',
Spiritus, 16, 61 (1975), pp. 427–35; J. Van Nieuwenhove in S. Urfer, Socialisme
et Eglise en Tanzanie (Paris, 1975), pp. 108–28.

7. President Kenyatta of Kenya in an address read to the plenary assembly
of AMECEA—the Association of Member Episcopal Conferences of Eastern
Africa—said 'we need the Church and ordinary Christians in our midst to tell
us when we are making a mistake. The Church is the conscience of society, and
today society needs a conscience. Do not be afraid to speak. If we go wrong
and you keep quiet, one day you may have to answer for our mistake',
AMECEA documentation service, 15 July 1976. With most of the channels of
information and key institutional cards in the party's hands, who but clerics are
in a position to play court jester let alone prophet in many African countries?
The susceptible seriousness with which prominent Africans take themselves is
already legendary in a continent once reputed for its carefree gaiety. Though
not unknown in traditional societies, political satire is conspicuously absent from
the contemporary African scene; cf. F. M. Rodegem, 'Ainsi parlait Saman-

dari', *Anthropos*, 69, 1974, pp. 753–835. Ironically enough for an organization associated with inquisitional intransigeance, the Church is perhaps the only body in a one-party setting able to see through prevailing myths such as that of a paradisal communalism ruined by the advent of egotistical colonialism.

8. One such exception is the archbishop of Lubumbashi's fearless denunciation of man's exploiting man (Lenten letter of 1976).

9. D. A. Barrett, 'Frontier situations for evangelization in Africa', *International Review of Mission*, 59 (1970), pp. 39–54 and W. Bühlmann, *La Terza Chiesa alle porte*, (Rome, 1975).

10. The International Labour Organization's report on Kenya noted that it was 'not the first to see parallels with the Latin American experience', IDOC dossier, *op. cit.*, p. 40. The Nigerian bishops at their plenary assembly 1976, felt obliged to remind their countrymen 'that affluence puts a special strain on ethical behaviour and right conduct'.

11. Mgr Nguyen van Binh, archbishop of Saigon, has endeavoured to convince his flock that egalitarian socialism is in theory preferable to exploitative capitalism and that the departure of priests and people to Vietnam's pioneering villages was not an unmitigated disaster.

12. Cf. FIDES, 4 April 1976 and 18 September 1976 (Rome); the confidential document describing the Roman Catholic Church as counter-revolutionary but counselling a cautious sapping from within rather than direct demolition, was later denounced as a forgery by one spokesman cf. *Informations Catholiques Internationales*, 15 May 1976.

13. AMECEA doc. service, Nairobi, 31 July 1976.

14. Text elaborated by Mgr Vieira Pinto and his clergy, July 1975 and translated from the Portuguese in IDOC bulletin 41, Rome 1976, p. 8. Cf. a similar text of Mgr Bakole, archbishop of Kananga, 'Zaïre in Church and Authenticity in Zaire', *Pro Mundi Vita* special note 39, (Brussels, 1975), p. 16.

15. ' "The Church of Christ" is truly present in all legitimate local congregations of the faithful which united with their pastors, are themselves called "churches" in the New Testament', says the AMECEA doc. service already quoted. The use of the term, which has Latin American parallels (cf. J. Marins, *La communidad eclesial de base*, Buenos Aires, 1969, pp. 37–42), is at least etymologically preferable to a broader use of the word as descriptive of collectivities or councils of particular Churches (cf. J. Mason 'The local Church', *SEDOS*, Rome 1975, pp. 395–96). It would be less mystifying as well as phenomenologically more exact and ecumenically more creditable if theologians were to speak of local (or particular) churches partially expressing rather than sacramentally embodying the Church as an ideal-type. Do particular cars sacramentalize automobility or do they restrictively reify the need for mobility? The danger of absolutizing institutions which witness to the Absolute has been underlined by H. Maurier, 'La théologie chrétienne des religions non-chrétiennes', *Lumen Vitae*, 31, 1 (1976), p. 93.

16. 'La vie des prêtres ne peut pas s'expliquer par la sacramentalisation ou l'animation d'une communauté chrétienne': Mgr Teissier, 'La vie d'une Eglise locale dans la perspective du synode épiscopal de 1974', *Revue des Sciences Religieuses*, 48, 4 (1974), p. 344.

F. Eboussi Boulaga

The African Christian in Search of Identity

CONFRONTED with a theme of this kind, one tends to feel a little queasy. The words used to state the topic are like so many obscure knots on a string: 'African, Christian, search, identity'. One feels as if an awful fog had come down behind the screen of a language whose plaything one is; one feels that one has to engage in some kind of evasive ritual, or to exorcize an unnameable yet obsessive and threatening presence. Instead of producing discourse which mediates between thought and practice, one proceeds as if paralyzed in advance, a prisoner of words loaded with myths and theoretical phantasmata. One is about to lose oneself in a verbal universe whose many words will be the reverse of meaningful silence on the questions with which we are besieged, and which relate to survival and everyday life, to decisions which concern most people's lives, and could involve them in collective disaster.

The flowers of our rhetoric grow on the dung-heap of dead things and disappointed hopes. Are we condemned to offer alibis, to intellectual prostitution or shadow boxing? A sense of this situation, and of the existential longing it evokes, is in the background as a disturbing presence throughout this article.

IDENTITY AND ADVENT

What is an African? Who is he? How and why is the question of his identity posed? There are two opposing viewpoints here. For the first, 'Africa' is merely a term for human realities which cannot be brought under one head. It stands for ecological diversity, ethnic differences and antagonisms, to which we must add social distance, and the economic and cultural distinctions introduced by colonists. There is also a suggestion of an abstract entity consisting of lacks: something without writing, states, industry or science. The African peoples are made to resemble one another in this kind of negative identity, in their common relegation to a prehistoric stage: a pre-industrial, pre-scientific and pre-philosophical phase. For the second viewpoint, the African identity is a fact (and evidence) of nature, and one maintained through the ages. Jeremiah bears witness to this when he asks if an Ethiopian can change his skin, or a leopard its spots. The so-called inadequacies of the African are of course only a reversed image of values and positive and immemorial qualities at the very basis of his culture and his being. Under the worst blows of fate, one notes the permanence of orality, universal symbolism, a metaphysics of vital force and of participation, of an innate sense of rhythm and of the sacred, of an aesthetics with a stable canon which celebrates life as a whole: life which is victorious over death.

These opposing theses do not refute one another, but enjoy the same premises. The identity with which they are both concerned belongs to the order of things, to the world of substrates. The African of which they talk is completely without historicity and the capacity to make himself, to provide himself with a new being. He is not a subject. Finally these images share a pre-critical naivety which obscures the real matter. The evolutionism behind the first viewpoint is the ideology which legitimizes the preponderance and cultural and political dominance of the West as a colonial force. Of course we have to escape from a vicious circle in which we are too concerned to pursue our quarrel with the master of yesterday, and too concerned at the same time to get his attention and win his interest, for we are still dependent on him.

The alchemist's search for a common African denominator is deceptive. It leads to a disembodied phantom, a form without substantial subjects. Identity is a pure determination of essence. There is no middle term which allows us to see how identity differs from itself in the characteristics with which we have to deal: how 'being' is attributable to other 'subjects', and can become their predicate; how 'Africanism' is these particular Africans before us.

The empirical approach to 'identity' is no more helpful. The results of socio-scientific inquiries and of ethnography can reach hardly any conclusions. Two complementary errors are at fault here: they concern a 'group' as a whole, and considered as such, the verified qualities and characters of some of its elements, and throw back on all the individuals (and on each of them) the properties of the aggregate that they go to make up. The value is that of an average which has to stand in statistical terms for the 'nature' of each instance. For these averages to have some weight and credibility, complete inventories are necessary. But that kind of exhaustive account is far from available. Even if we managed to produce one, it would be of little value. Reality would have changed in the meantime.

What we can describe is a set of conditions, suasions and facts. However important and necessary they may be, they mean nothing apart from what men make of them, and the ways in which they make their denstinies fit together. Factual data and suasions have no reality outside a project which determines them. The colour of the skin, geography, close or similar ways of life, do not prescribe solidarity and a common destiny. For centuries, these 'facts' have left blacks in a state of dispersion, in a state of indifference or hostility towards one another or towards others. They were not objective factors of a common way of being in the world and a collective self-consciousness.

The African has a birthday. His is the unprecedented advent of men for whom Africa is the location of their introduction into the world; for whom this 'race', this space, these ways of life, these traditions and these histories are the conditions for their emergence as members of an historical subject; and for a collective initiative with its own self-avowal and advance. The African is not defined in terms of these ethnic data, these forests and these savannas, or these costumes; he gives himself these things. He has to appropriate them for himself by transforming them.

The African has no actual content; he exists with a specific location only if he adopts his physical, biological, cultural and historical conditioning factors. To adopt is to take self-responsibility, as if for that which is not self; it is to discover that one was, that one still is, outside oneself, alien to oneself; that one has therefore to rediscover oneself and transform oneself, to become what one was not: the will and capacity to act from a certain starting-point, in a direction decided by this situation in space, time and human experience, but which one has chosen and now invents together with others. We have to assess this transformation which favours an individual of startling novelty which the past in no way determines, even though it might have moulded him before. Continuity is no longer something proper to representations of life, schemes of action, instances of loyalty to the tribal tradition. There is nothing to copy, to reproduce. What is in question is a new beginning, the creation of new human relations, of new ways of life, of new cultures.

THE BLACK: THE AFRICAN AND CHRISTIANITY

With the arrival of African self-determination, Christianity takes on a new shape. It lives in the world of dead things and beings of yesterday which condition the present but do not determine it any longer, at least directly, awaiting their meaning from the present intention of the people alive today, from this perspective which endows existing things with a dimension which can mobilize being as a whole.

Colonial Christianity will not evade reinterpretation, or escape being remoulded, and even destroyed or rejected. Retrospectively (that is to say, from the end which it ordains for itself, from the meaning which it makes and towards which he is advancing, the African cannot avoid a total view of black Christianity as a form of alienated belief which is typically apparent when consciousness, detached from the worldly realities which it adopted and by means of which it was mediated, has become alien to itself. The world to which it is attached, the object of its belief, then appears as *other* to its world: as its abstraction or inversion. The religion of the black, beginning exactly where he deserts himself as subject and loses the support of his judgment and of reality, takes on the form of an alien being without any point of reference, which is apparent in an authoritarian fashion not in terms of content but of external form. Christianity is welcomed in the position it occupies in encounter, in the status that it enjoys and the functions that it fulfils, and for the forces that it represents or symbolizes in the eyes of the black.

The African has another understanding of Christianity. He sees it in the dimension of history, in its temporal and spatial aspects, with its variations, its diversity, and also its civil warfare. Still less is the black able to locate himself in the vast genesis of man; in his vast millenarian quest for a total meaning connected with his experiences, his ways of accommodating, producing or mastering his environment. He is unaware of the pointless conflicts of religions or ideologies with a universal claim but factual reference. Suspecting a possible discontinuity between doctrine and practice, he does not see how Christianity could lend itself to manipulation, to the profit of the powers that be, of racial and civilizing mythologies, to the service of nationalist or individual passions, of fear and cowardice and relentless spiritual alienation. He has not yet witnessed the effects of the symbolic domination which introduces guilt to human existence, and wipes out individual conscience and judgment and the will to self-emancipation: the will not to live by proxy, and the will to run the risks of truth. He cannot face the jungle of a world changed by five centuries of expansion of the Christian West. The Christian ethic, centred on individual salvation and an affirmation of its monopoly of truth, has shown its impotence, its inadequacy, and sometimes its passive and active complicity, in the face of immense passions and forces of institutionalized and planetary destruction.

The African senses or knows all that and many other things. More than the content of this knowledge and experience, it is the understanding of historical perspective which structures his awareness and organizes his perception of Christianity. He cannot see it other than from the spot he occupies, where he is trying to create meaning. In relation to its originating bodies, black Christianity must seem wrapped in naivety and without historic freedom.

Christianity has matured and educated the blacks who produced what you call Africans. That is undeniable. Who could reasonably deny it? Christianity and the missionaries did everything for the blacks, but they did not make the African, who begins with a decision to reject this paternalism and the context of ignorance and violence where this kindness towards him is exercised. Even if he is a child of the mission, he has to die to his childhood in order to become a father in his turn, the head of a new line of men, but not in order to perpetuate the negroes, colonizable objects of indoctrination and charity.

In order to describe the African I could have drawn on literature. There the African moulded by history inquires into his 'identity' and into Christianity, asking what is to be done with it now. I shall cite only the epilogue of *Down Second Avenue* by the South African writer Ezechiel Mphahlele. The reference of what he says there can be extended. His first conviction is that henceforth there is no room for anyone who wants to run the African's life from outside in the name of an absolute knowledge and dominant mission. He says that he believes that nothing allows the white man to tell him how to run his social life, or to run it for him. Africa is no longer for the white man who refuses to learn and comes only to teach. The Gospel does not authorize religious imperialism or spiritual dependence. Nor does it authorize the activism of the offer of salvation, the indiscreet proselytism, which does violence to conscience, and takes souls by storm in order to submit them to control and domination. Mphahlele says that all his life people have been getting at his soul, pulling it in every direction. He has been used by enthusiastic evangelists, by brutal police surveillance. So many hands have been stretched out towards him and so many voices have assailed his ears with the crazy rhythm of a train in motion that he has to cry out: Leave me alone!

The African is tired of the zeal which seeks to conquer. He needs peace in order to find freedom of spirit and face what he holds most at heart, which will be no wallowing in individualism, for his personal life is too closely bound up with the collective drama. Mphahlele says that he is still angry about poverty, injustice and the legal oppression of the little people by the strong. He is immunized against everything that does not attack these evils and oppression. He is tired of a certainty which is too self-satisfied. He says that he admires men like Bach who can express their religious faith succinctly. Meaning for us can arise from the unexpected, from a series of events where we seem pulled by destiny. We find Christian triumphalism appalling, all the more because Christianity and the churches are anachronistic in view of the harsh realities of the present. In a situation in which a powerful Herrenvolk or master race made the law for three centuries to the sole profit of the master race, and where people have been oppressed because of their race, the Church has tried to apply out-of-date ideas, insisting on the infinite value of the individual soul, looking only for guarantees and concessions for individuals, avoiding the necessity and responsibility for mass actions, and remaining careless of political realities. Faced with the calculated violence of the hereditary bearers of Christianity, it has engaged in no missionary action. The new barbarians were not evangelized; only the 'savages' received the attention and care of the apostles. For us, says, Mphahlele, the Church has become the symbol of the dishonesty of the West. What meaning is left in a Christianity reduced to a formal organization of gestures, rites and behaviours which have no end other than to signify belonging? None. Christianity is like a screen between the African and the others, a distorting prism, a pre-emption of his freedom to see other cultures and ways of life, as they see themselves and understand themselves. It is a super-ego which judges and censures before knowing. It is necessary to rediscover freedom to look and to experiment; openness to the universal aspect, to the many-sided fulness of human life and history. In Mphahlele it is the African and not the Negro who speaks; for any responsible African intellectual, South Africa is an enlarging mirror which enables him to see the logical outcome of tendencies and premisses which seem anodyne and innocent. Remember that Christianity in itself exists only as a limit-concept, like a state of nature; it is not met with other than in a particular condition, an historical instance, even though its supra-temporal idea plays a necessary and enlivening regulative rôle—which it can and should play. Far from being an excuse, it is that idea which authorizes judgment and the critical spirit. Therefore it is no block to responsibility or barrier to understanding. Christianity cannot deprive us of our historical and cultural self-determination.

CHRISTIANITY AFRICAN-STYLE

What will it be like, this cut-to-measure Christianity, sensitive to the heart and soul of the African? To what extent will it still be an obedience of faith and unconditional submission to the sovereign authority of the Word of God? How will it escape destructive heresy, syncretism and relativism? These urgent questions are unavoidable, even if it is impossible to give a full answer here.

What we are trying now to recover in our exercise of freedom, what we are trying to 'inform' as far as we are able, is the great chaos which underlies the language of orthodoxy, once outside the closed field of ethical conformism and Christian dogmatism. It is only in the void brought about by the latter's inadequacy that the African can think and think and act. Faith is not, or rather ought not to be, an inert mode of common reference. The mere possession of a creed, of the same articles, the same formulas, the one 'salvation' which comes from the one faith, the one grace and the one Christ, have not broken down the wall of separation and opposition between man and woman, slave and freedman, believer and pagan. They have not prevented slavery, racial and economic discrimination, the excesses of the lust of the eyes, of the flesh, and the presumption of the spirit. In his Word God proclaims himself as that illimitable power which operates within divisions and conflicts in order to overcome them, like an act of reconciliation. It shows itself as the creative power of love which allows self-consistent things to be as they are and causes individuals to emerge full of self-understanding where other men wish to enslave them to idols, to sacrifice them to the Law or to Tradition, to the demons of the blood, of sex and power, or riches. Outside this new creation which is under way, the proclamation of biblical revelation becomes chat, lyrical incantations, the religion of the word. The obsession of orthodoxy or biblicism becomes an alibi and the index of a spiritual neuroticism. The same is true of syncretism. There is no paradox or easy irony in saying that syncretism is sure to arise where collections of sacred objects, rites or institutions are handed on; where the present and the future are rejected in the name of a substantial holding acquired or inherited from the past. Meanings lodged in the code of Scripture, traditions, dogmas, the Reformers' books, are not meant to stay intact. If they are calcified, they can only turn in on themselves, grow corrupt and become ingredients in vile mixtures. Syncretism is the fate of all truth which sees itself as a content, a localizable deposit; of all that rejects the paschal need to die in order to rise again, and is content with illusory 'syntheses' and 'symbioses'. We can see why the African is ready to leave the dead to bury their dead.—But you, come, follow me on the roads you will make yourself; withstanding the shock of the future, that of the God who is coming.

Let us not be afraid of that other paper tiger, relativism. Christianity is not absolute. It does not live a separate existence in some heaven of ideas in themselves. It is relative to an historical humanity. More simply, it is always the Christianity of someone and for someone, the Christianity of an age and for that age. It exists only through men and for men. If they were not there, it would not exist, and that is true of each generation. It takes its origin in specific events in the life of a unique individual, in his death. It is contained in time and history. It relativizes the absolute; and we do not know what the absolute is but what it is not, and what relation it has with the rest. Even Christianity only expresses the relation that the world and man have with God, not knowing or speaking of him in any other way than under the form of that relation. It does not follow that all religions are as good as one another. That would contradict the weight that an African gives to localizations in time and space, which are not interchangeable but as integral parts of meaning as its condition and its limit. To 'know one's limit is to sacrifice oneself', like some imaginary almighty power, universal indetermination or abstraction; like a direct universality. The African would offend against his 'tradition' and his experience of historicity if he tried to elevate his Christianity into a general norm, if he thought of it as the only authentic religion, as the only way to be fully human and to relate to God. He does not have to choose between the absolutization of his beliefs, his practices, his way of life and the levelling out of all opinions and of all values. The truth is his to make, here and now; he cannot make it for anyone else, and no one can take his place. To sacrifice oneself is to let others arrive as persons, it is to agree to an advent through them in their difference. The internal criterion for the legitimation of a specific Christianity is this standing-down in order to receive oneself from others, while becoming the food of life for others.

Christianity African-style will not start from a search for the 'essence of Christianity'. Having encountered it as a social and historical entity, the African will establish the rules of its correct usage, the system of relations which he allows to be set up with the rest. He will ask how Christianity makes it possible to express the human condition in the economy of existence, so as to hold back the forces of egotism and arbitrariness. He opens up a field of possible transformation of existence which allows life to be organized other than in accordance with the old formulas of resentment, fear and oppressive violence, and which offers the radical emancipation of all men.

The 'theology' arising from this procedure will not be absolute in any

way. It will be a finished performance, well within the infinite competence of all Christians of yesterday, today and tomorrow, since it will
employ a knowledge of this world and of this mankind, of human
relations which are independent of the 'facts of revelation' (which gives
those facts a context in which to become intelligible and livable).

In order to transform these demands into programmes, we have to
return to our starting-point; to climb out of our abysses of silence; to
make the essential *you* speak that has been mute under the mass of
propaganda and general laxity. We have to be willing to die in order to
be reborn somewhere else, somewhere far away.

Translated by J. Maxwell

Jacob Medéwalé Agossou

The Demands of the Gospel and African Anthropology

> 'A society does not change its ethics merely by chang-
> ing its rules. To alter its ethics, its principles must be
> different . . . Any change of ethics constitutes a revo-
> lutionary change'.[1]

THE conflicts between the demands of 'Christian morality' and those of 'customary law' constitute a daily problem for a large number of baptized Africans. What follows is an attempt to stimulate thought on two aspects of this problem. The first is the difference between the demands of the Gospel and a kind of Christian morality which is a system of 'socio-logical' rules derived from the history of western behaviour. The second is the conflict between this morality and African ethics, itself based on the antithesis of life and death, with all the variations on that theme.

In order to see the problem more clearly it may be useful to begin by outlining the areas of conflict.

THE AREAS OF CONFLICT

Today it is not rare that one meets African Christians who are exposed to veritable dramas of conscience when faced with problems of marriage, economics, religious beliefs, political options, and so on. Topics for reflection and research, such as 'traditional African beliefs and Christian faith', "traditional economy and development", 'traditional African values and conversion', 'African socialism and Western socialism', etc., rouse much and even passionate interest everywhere.

From the 'man in the street' of our African towns to the most isolated peasant in our far-flung villages where, exposed to a ruthless climate and with his primitive technique, he extracts his daily pittance from the earth, his mother and foster-mother, there is practically nobody any more who does not wonder how to reconcile African beliefs and ritual practices with the demands of some kind of modernization which have arisen from the encounter with different cultural systems. The educated African looks for solutions but examines his own position in the process.[2] Should one simply break the links with other cultural groups and live in a kind of autarchy, of a far more social and cultural nature than a simple economic one? What would be the chances of such an option and how long would it survive? And what if one opts for throwing open all the doors to the West and its value-system, which arrived and installed itself in force, and which is there in spite of political independence, and impose this on the gradual destruction of our best-tried institutions? Is it factually and rightly true that westernization and modernization are one and the same thing? If this is so, why has the modern black man to suffer conflicts, crises and being torn apart?[3] These questions arise

—at the level of the institution which is as old as mankind, namely, the family;
—at the level of both economics and politics;
—at the level of beliefs and social-religious ritual;
—in short, at the particular level of the 'demands of Christian morality' and the 'customary laws and habits' of the Africans.
Why should this happen?

When the African élite considers these questions, the wise man, the old one, the true guardian of beliefs and practices several centuries old, will meditate and try to sort out what is happening through a contemplation based on prayer.

When the lines of questioning and meditating cross, can one see clear enough to say exactly what has to be done? When the interior dramas, referred to above, are embedded in the practice of everyday life, does this not mean that, because of their integration in society and their Christian codification, the moral values have to be re-examined in the light of the Demands of the Gospel and of African Anthropology?

THE DEMANDS OF THE GOSPEL AND 'CHRISTIAN MORALITY'

In par. 15 of the Decree on the Church's Missionary Activity the second Vatican Council states as characteristic features of Christianity the *promotion of universal love* among men, and the *new law*, defined in the commandment of brotherly love, embracing all our fellow men, including our enemies. But this does not yet show the radical novelty. The novelty lies, not so much in that sense of humanity, recognized and respected in every human being, as in the statement that Christ is the foundation-stone of this universal inter-human love. The practical and concrete realization of this belief is achieved through charity, in the sense of *agapè*, i.e., in the radical orientation of a reality of divine origin. This is grafted into us through the gift of the Spirit, promised and already present in all that are baptized (I Cor. 3:5). Now, this gift of a 'new birth' is said to be the source of a powerful driving-force towards communion which is given concrete shape in the call of all as well as the welcoming of all in Christ. And when this acceptance meets with differences, neither foreseen nor wished-for, this spiritual force is also able to drive Christians towards reconciliation.

This demand of agapè is, finally, also a source of personalization, through which everyone is an unprecedented eternal achievement in solidarity with the community. The Good and Happiness, put to us by these demands of the Gospel, find their original codification, bluntly framed and both painful and concise, in the Sermon on the Mount (Mt. 5:3–13).

These demands are the principles. They are the ideal which, as in the case of any society, lay down the basic general ideas without spelling out the ways in which these principles can be applied to concrete situations.

And here it is the connection between the ideal and the positive, concrete applications determined by some 'Christian morality', which constitutes the problem. Within the limits of this article I can only deal with three kinds of difficulties:

—the complexity of the human being and the socio-cultural situation in which he has to live;
—the identification of the Gospel's command to love one's neighbour with the conventional morality of a Christian society;
—the lack of faithfulness among Christians themselves to the substance of their faith.

The Complexity of the Human Being and the Socio-Cultural Situation in Which He Has to Live

At this point the famous dictum of St Augustine, so often quoted, 'Ama et fac quod vis' (love and do as you want to), is not exactly one of the most practical pieces of advice. It is important to explain what is meant by human nature and a human being by a serious analysis of his social situation. We all know that, because of circumstances of time and place, this social situation ignores the simplicity of the Gospel's ideal which it is supposed to embody. Any human society is essentially fragile and subject to change. As Dr Kwame Nkrumah has written: 'To say that circumstances change is a truism. It nevertheless has a point. It means in fact, that if one wants to apply the ideal throughout the vicissitudes of life it may be necessary to modify or replace the institutions so that the same ideal can be effectively pursued. There are no particular institutions which can exclusively thrive on the ideal, regardless of local conditions. All institutions must be imbued with pragmatism'.[4]

This means that changes in existing social situations bring with them changes in the institutions. In the specific case of the western expression of Christianity, Christian moral thought was bound to borrow from the philosophies prevailing in the cultures in which it developed. Thus Stoicism, then neo-Platonism and a little later Aristotelianism, all contributed more than some basic ideas to this development. The whole vision of the universe, of living beings and things at large, which characterised these cultures provided this Christian development with the framework for its thought, including its protology and its teleology. In the process the first enthusiasm and evangelical fervour were soon exhausted for lack of contact with the source. This is hardly astonishing. 'As long as a law remains true, i.e., rooted in the biological, social and religious reality, there is less danger that its basic intent gets lost because there is an objective continuity between the original attitude and the particular direction of its application. But it is no longer the same in the case of purely positive laws which require mental gymnastics to make their observance correspond to the spirit in which they were generally laid down. This tends to be more easily forgotten the more these laws multiply and their execution becomes difficult. The result is that the material execution of the precept becomes an end in itself and that, in the mind of the one who applies the law, it becomes more important to *have satisfied* than to practise it. To refer to the case of the Pharisees, it is then more important to *have paid* the tithe than *to pay it:* that is unquestionably the sign that the particular precept has become an end in itself and is no longer seen as a way of fulfilling "hic et nunc" the will of God.'[5]

In such circumstances those that hold on to a morality that is closer to the source will not be long in coming forward. This is confirmed by ancient Israel, the history of the Church, and again in our own time. The debate continues. And it is here that the second difficulty arises.

The Confusion between the Demand of the Gospel that We Must Love Our Neighbour and the Social Morality of a Christian Society

It is not enough to provide definitions of what is good, and what are rights and duties. We must also know how love can actively inspire the restraints and behaviour laid down by decree in the subjects concerned. Moral good depends on a system of values. The value of an action is judged by the fact of its role in a system. We call good what can be integrated, bad what does not fit in with what is already constituted or accepted. It is here that one should shy away from hasty identifications: for instance, one cannot *ipso facto* identify the Gospel's commandment to love the neighbour with the social morality of a way of life, even in a Christian society. The moral ideas about the good maintain quite rightly that, in spite of the transcendence of the good, the priority of values must be rationally established. This means that it must be integrated in a general order of the universe and based on the real, social and religious character of human nature. On this point one has to recognize that, in Europe, the Church, as the inspiration and guardian of moral behaviour, has not failed to assist in spreading the previous values implied in the dignity of the human person, in concern for the most poor and for peace, and so on.

Nevertheless, the same Church has not always succeeded in avoiding the pitfalls of legalism, moralism and sociological conformism. This fault has further consequences when, under cover of evangelical demands, one introduces distant and simple peoples to what are in fact only socio-cultural side-effects of a European environment as if the particular applications of the same moral principles must be formulated and practised everywhere and at all times in a uniform and univocal way. It is obvious that even when two societies share the same moral principles they formulate different rules for their application. In the words of Dr Kwame: 'In Israel the ass was so important that God judged it necessary in regulating human relationships to mention the ass explicitly in a moral rule: "You shall not covet your neighbour's ass". If God deigned to lay down an equivalent rule for us he would certainly forbid us to covet our neighbour's car, not his ass. In this case God would lay down a new moral rule meant to ensure the application of an unchanged moral principle, taking into account life as it is led today'.[6]

This lack of respect for the socio-cultural realities of peoples to whom proud and valiant missionaries went out to bring the good news, this contempt for those of a different culture, aggravated by Catholics' own infidelity to the contents of the belief they profess, leads us to the third difficulty.

The Catholics' Infidelity to the Contents of their Faith

Here, reference to two sacraments will suffice to illustrate what I mean. In this regard one can briefly point out some features due to the development that took in Christian sensitivity. The two sacraments referred to are baptism and penance.

At the beginning, when the great effusions of the Spirit which, according to the Acts of the Apostles took place in the first days, had come to an end, Christian baptism lost its impetus. The ideal which it expressed made little appeal and catechumens only too readily postponed the sacrament in the strict sense to the end of their life. Their Christian identity card, signed uncompleted on their joining the catechumenate, could well remain uncompleted till the final moment: death. Fortunately, this was not the case with everybody. Christian people tried, as well as they could, to obey the rigorous demands of a morality which was far more characterized by Stoicism than by the Gospel.

In these conditions the sacrament of penance was considered to be for extreme cases. Reality showed that all Christians were not saints, and they were well aware of it. The strong sense of sin brought about a multiplication of the rules of fasting and of pilgrimages to holy places.

While during this whole period the mass of ordinary believers were looking for the springs of grace and salvation, theology spent itself on sterile theorizing about the relations between human nature, grace and sin. To admit that one was a sinner became a formalistic habit and a way of eluding one's real moral responsibilities. Should one then not speak of a critical situation, a crisis affecting that high moral sense implied in baptism with the radical change it should bring about with it in the moral conduct of the neophyte? This state of affairs must have gradually taken root, doubtless because of Christians' own infidelity to the content of their faith. Was this actual crisis in the sense of sin, the sacrament of penance, confession, or reconciliation—as it is no longer very clear how to describe it—not the sign of a general mediocrity, a general disarray of the individual conscience in the face of changes which had actually taken place? Or should one see it as the expression of the need to learn again the positive content of loving the neighbour and the Sermon on the Mount (Mt 5:7) and whether finally the time had come for the western expression of Christian morality to listen again to the demands of the Gospel? For, whatever society man lives in, the demands of the Gospel remain for all time the primal source: 'If man but knew the gift of God' (Jn 4).

AFRICAN ANTHROPOLOGY AND CHRISTIAN MORALITY

When, at the end of the last century and the beginning of this one, western Christianity brought its light to the poor pagans of Africa, 'seated in the shadow of idolatry and in the darkness of ignorance' *(sic)*, the three difficulties outlined above constituted already a real malignant tumour in an age-worn organism. We know that only life can give, support and preserve life. True, according to an appropriate theology, the sacramental rite of baptism, once conferred, endowed the new convert 'automatically' with divine life. The palpable signs of this radical change were a white dress made for the occasion at the cost of much sacrifice and saving and a new name with an 'overseas' ring to it. The newness of this complete nominal change of course in a white dress did not go beyond that. That Zouménou is henceforth called Sylvan, and Yéhinou, Susan, changes absolutely nothing, not even nominally, when we know that in this case Zouménou and Sylvan mean exactly the same thing: a man born or living in the forest, and that Yéhinou and Susan are also the same. Where, in all this, is the 'newness' implied in the acceptance of the Gospel?

Look at the questions included in the baptismal ritual:

Q.: What do you ask of God's Church?

A.: The faith.

Q.: What does the faith give you?

A.: *Eternal life*.

In spite of the simple wording this last answer implies a whole programme, the unity of which depends on the unity of *life*. The life, described here as eternal, is promised through the faith. Now, for the black African such a project constitutes the finality of all finalities. *His vision of the world is derived from it; his socio-religious institutions* encourage its advent, development and conservation, and his system of values is based on it.[7]

Life in the World-View of the Black

A world-view is a way of thinking which looks at everything and looks for some understanding of reality as a whole. It is an interpretation of the world, a more or less explicit answer to ultimate questions about the origin and purpose of man's life, even if this answer is agnostic, such as: we cannot know the origin and end of the world. A world-view is therefore not just a 'representation of the world' as it exists. It tries to draw what is possible from the core of what is real. It is based on a self, in the individual and collective sense. Such a 'self' is the total personality. That is why a world-view embraces the values, ideas and practical options through which an individual or a group asserts itself. It is neither necessarily nor totally conscious. And this is why, ultimately, it shows itself rather as a belief than as knowledge.

The concept of life according to the world-view of the Fon of Benin (formerly Dahomey) may be best approached by looking at the dual relationships between:

A. Gbe/Gbeto: Life-World/Man

B. Gbeto/Gbedoto: Man/God the Creator

All other relationships are derived from these two: man/things; man/spirit, and so on, and one can see that existence is dominated by *three major constants:*

Gbe: Life-World
Gbeto: Man
Gbedoto: God or the founding principle of this world.

Man vibrates with the desire to live, a desire which arises from his awareness of an immortal principle, which is immanent in himself: Se. It is a desire to live, but in such a way as to give concrete expression to a word. This is the word of life, a kind of enigma which every man carries in himself and of which the authorized interpretation belongs to the soothsayer (Fakanto). Once it has been made explicit, this word must be lived during one's life-time through the gradual dialectical process of living participation. Within this participation man constantly discovers that his true life begins beyond death in the full participation with the source of life, i.e., God.

Human life, as animated and animating breath, appears to the Fon as a promise of plenitude which fulfils itself progressively within the framework of existence, directed towards God, in whom the Fon see the principle on which the reality of 'world-life' is founded. All the social institutions contribute through a detailed 'instruction' towards the establishment of this global vision. Here we shall deal only with the 'Vodun', which is the word for religion.

The 'Vodun'

'Vodun' is first of all the Benin word for religion. Religion, taken here as the religious behaviour of the Fon in so far as it can be observed, is an attempt to find the answer to the ultimate questions of life and existence. It is a language in the anthropological sense of the word. This means that the Vodun presents itself as a socio-cultural system which is meant to be complete. The ultimate meaning of the Vodun phenomenon is life in search of the fulness of living. The 'Vodunsi' (the Vodun believer) is wholly bound up with an integrated vision of the world. This vision is demanded by the transcendence which is immanent in us, on the one hand in the form of 'Se' and on the other by the call of life to life. To renounce this integration and this dynamic and vital expansion is to renounce life. Like everybody else, the Fon instinctively rejects this idea. The Fon is so attached to life that in his language 'to live' means 'to eat life'. This means that anything that contributes to the birth, development and preservation of life is a 'chewing of life'. In short, we may say that man desires life; he is aware of it in himself in the immanence of the 'saved' which dwells in him, and he uses everything to achieve his total fulfilment in him who is by definition seen as the source of all life. This is why our logic and our 'social-logical' demand that the urge towards life should be widely supported by our system of values even in the least important particular applications of it.

Life and the Rules of Custom

Moral rules define the values which must be respected, developed and submitted to. These moral values have three basic features: they are *transcendent, immanent* and there are *priorities*. A value is essentially something which is beyond the level of straightforward facts, and this in the sense that there is no way of reaching values by a continuous movement of facts. All the elements of moral conscience imply going beyond natural tendencies, spontaneous sensibilities and simple judgements of fact. This means that if the natural order prepares us for and points to the order of moral values, there is nevertheless no continuity from the one to the other. Yet, although transcendent, values are also called immanent because they respond to the demands of our conscience and to certain aspirations of our spirit; as such they can be the object of our love, our enthusiasm and our commitment. But, in isolation, one value has not much importance. Values are interrelated in a certain order and with a certain cohesion, in short, there is a 'scale of values'. This scale goes up and goes down. In the same way as the false is opposed to the true, the beautiful to the ugly, so the morally right is opposed to the morally wrong.

Between the two poles there is an upward and a downward movement which makes one moral act more or less meritorious and an offence more or less serious. The orders and prohibitions contained in customary rule are subject to the same three criteria. What is special in our context is that here everything is based on the duality of life and death, and not on that of being and nothingness.

Anything encouraging birth, development and fruitfulness in life is deemed to be 'good', while anything damaging to life is declared as 'evil' (Gbesu). This is the basis on which any application at any level is based. If it is forbidden to eat this or that (this animal, that fish, that vegetable, etc.) the reason is that in ultimate terms, life is protected by this particular alimentary abstinence. Sexual prohibitions operate on the same basis. The purification required of the woman who has just given birth, or concerning touching the dead, etc., have the same end in view. Everything is based on the fact that life and the care for life influence all human actions. The good, the evil, the true and the false are judged in terms of life. This is our kind of logic, a logic for life, demanding a corresponding sense of morality. This call of life to life appeals to the message of the sermon on the mount and to love understood as agapè.

LOVE AND SANCTIONS—LIFE AND PROHIBITIONS

The conflicts, then, between the demands made by a particular Christian morality now appear to be far more serious than at a first glance. It is much less a matter of superficial particular institutions than a matter of the source of its principles. The oppositions revealed by these contrasts may be formulated as the contrast between love and sanctions on the one hand, and life and prohibition on the other.

To the degree in which the law of love and life proclaimed by Christ is turned into a legal code of 'does' and 'don'ts' which has developed in a particular society, one can understand that such a code cannot adequately meet and be applied to every single socio-cultural environment. If we agree that love, in the Christian sense, and life as we have just described it according to the way the African looks at things, are 'good' at the most important level, we will understand that these two realities may provide a common ground for specific applications without, for all that, accepting that there are two different moralities. For, indeed, the moral sense of a society does not change simply by the imposition of 'laws'. If morals have to change, the principles have to change. Yet, the appeal of the Gospel to love and life corresponds profoundly with the aspirations of all peoples and particularly with those of the blacks who look for a communal brotherhood and for living together in peace.

Has the time come, perhaps, to learn again how to listen to life so that we can love it better and with such rules as should serve it?

Translated by Theo Weston

Notes

1. Dr Kwame Nkrumah, *Consciencism* (London, n.d.).
2. Jacob Agossou, 'Voies africaines de la thélogie', in *Vie Eudiste,* vol. I, no. 5, December 1972.
3. Isidore de Souza, 'Pouvons-nous rester Africains et Chrétiens', in *Telema,* December 4, 1975.
4. Dr Kwame Nkrumah, *op. cit.* (Paris, 1975).
5. Jean L'Hour, in *La Morale de l'Alliance.*
6. Dr Kwame Nkrumah, *ibid.*
7. Jacob Agossou, *Gbeto et Gbedoto* (Paris, 1972).

Jean-Marc Ela

Ecclesial Ministry and the Problems of the Young Churches

NO inquiry into the ministry can be made outside the framework of ecclesiology: our deepened theological understanding of the data of exegesis and history obliges us to refer to the Church as the locus of all Christian inquiry and attention to the word of God in the present circumstances of the world and of history. Any living theology must therefore take account of the major preoccupations and serious demands of the various communities of believers. With this in mind, I want to reconsider the question of ministries, seeing it in the light of the problems faced by young churches at the present time.

The renewal of the theology of ministries following Vatican II demonstrates the need to rediscover the Holy Spirit as the principle for resolving the theological problem of the ministry. Indeed, a careful reading of the Acts of the Apostles reminds us that there is no ministry except in the Spirit.

In returning to the theology of the Spirit, the Council did not merely point out the limitations of a theology of the ministry dominated by a juridical thinking tending towards a clerical centralization; it also brought into question the whole concept of a monolithic ministry, by recognizing a diversity of ministries more in conformity with apostolic tradition. Vatican II stressed the need for a multiplicity of ministries. One has only to read the following: 'Various kinds of services are required that the Church may be planted and the Christian community grow. These services—raised up by divine calling from among the congregation of the faithful itself—should be diligently fostered and developed by all. Among them are the offices of priests, deacons and catechists, and Catholic Action. Similarly, either by their prayer or active work, religious of both sexes render indispensable service (*officium*) in making the kingdom of Christ take root in souls, giving it a firmer footing there and spreading it still further'.[1]

The continuing relevance of these words is obvious; they call for a reassessment of the ministry in the light of a fresh look at the relationship between the Spirit and the Church. The recognition of diverse ministries is linked with the fundamental fact that the ministry is first and foremost a shared responsibility of the Church as a whole; it is an actualization of the ministry of Christ in the Spirit. To affirm the diversity of ministries is a reference to the Spirit who continually inspires the faithful, in so many different forms, with a desire to work for the service of the Church in this or that particular sphere. For it is the Spirit who is the source of these ministries in all their diversity. What we see in the different forms of service in the Church is the Spirit at work. It is he who 'distributes his gifts as he will for the common good'.[2] And accepting that the Church needs different ministries means admitting that what has up to now seemed a kind of 'clerical tyranny' must come to an end.

In fact, though it touched upon the problems presented by the ministry and life of the priesthood today, the Council did not make priests the centre of its search for a renewal to confront the difficulties attendant on present-day apostolic work in Christian communities. All it had to say about charismata makes that clear. Furthermore, in the text just quoted, we have seen how, in the examples it gives of various ministries, the Council mentions catechists and Catholic Action as well as priests and deacons; it places the work of the religious orders in the same sphere of ecclesial activity. It is thus legitimate to consider all these various ways of serving the Church as authentic ministries. In effect, the Council's move towards studying the theology of the laity came up against a view of the problem of ministries centred around the priestly ministry as the only one. For Vatican II, not merely were the 'clergy' not adequate by themselves—they were not equipped at all to respond to the new needs of the Church. To follow the spirit of the Council, we must return again to the Decree on the Apostolate of the Laity. Indeed it seems an impossibility to discuss ministries in the Church apart from a theology of the laity. The rediscovery of the laity was a reminder that the Christian ministry is not wholly contained by its institutional form. In other words, any renewed reflexion on the ministry must include the laity as well. For lay people too have their share of responsibility in the apostolic functions undertaken by the Church as a whole. 'The existence of every layman', declared the Council, 'is at the same time a witness and a living instrument of the

Church's mission "according to the measure of Christ's gift" (Eph 4:7)'.[3] And, more concretely, 'The Hierarchy . . . is not the only agency through which [Christ] performs his prophetic task. . . . He uses the laity too'.[4]

In short, 'the apostolate of the laity is a share in the Church's mission of salvation. By baptism and confirmation all are assigned to this apostolate by the Lord himself'.[5] As we see, then, the Council went beyond an earlier theology of the apostolate of the laity which tried to reduce what primarily flows from the life of baptism to no more than a delegated function from the hierarchy. It rejected the notion of a 'mandate' from the bishops. In doing so, it clearly recognized the special nature of the ministries of laypeople: they are not just an extension of the ministry of the hierarchy, and do not therefore need to be marked by a rite modelled on episcopal or priestly ordination. It may well be good to have liturgical acts to consecrate the ministry of the laity in the community[6], but it is important to avoid making rules that involve any risk of clericalization. For instance, the laying-on of hands is necessary only for ordination to the institutional ministry. At all events, it is clear that the present trend is to integrate laypeople into ministries within their own Christian communities. Though many people have reservations about it, the Roman document *Ministeria quaedam*, establishing (alongside the diaconate) ministries that laypeople can undertake without receiving any kind of ordination, illustrates that trend. Certain comments that this situation provokes may open new lines of study in relation to the difficulties facing the young churches.

We may start from one decisive point: the new understanding of the Church brought out by Vatican II involves a far greater awareness of the ecclesial significance of the Christian ministry. Furthermore, the fresh light cast on all ministry in the Church by the theology of the Spirit shows up far more clearly the place of the laity and their role in the ministerial structure of the Church. In this new light, it is no longer possible to make fitness for the ministry a purely clerical preserve by relating every act of ministry to the laying-on of hands. A redistribution of ministries is demanded both by present-day ecclesiology and by the Biblical theology of charismata. It should not, however, be looked on as 'a temporary measure of conservation'; it is not a matter of entrusting to laypeople certain deputizing functions where clergy are lacking. This is no novelty, but a return to a past when the 'power of order' was the sole criterion for the Church's ministry. It might be said that wanting to turn the laity into no more than the auxiliaries of the clergy means that one is taking seriously neither the charisma given to every member of the Church, nor, ultimately, the Spirit who is the source of all ministry.[7]

We know today that baptism and confirmation give laypeople a sphere of action in the Church. Failure to recognize the importance of those two sacraments created a clericalism which denied them any ministerial role. The question is whether we are not still, unconsciously, victims of this mentality when we come to consider possible solutions to the problem of the shortage of priests in the young churches.

It appeared that the restoration of the diaconate would put an end to some of the difficulties faced by dioceses with too few priests. Then it seemed that a reconsideration of celibacy—thought to be one of the barriers to more priestly vocations in the modern world—would result in the ordaining of married men. At the present time, indeed, this solution is seen by many people as the last hope for the young churches, and they cling to the idea even though the 1972 Roman Synod would not grant episcopal conferences the right to admit married men to the priesthood. Though Paul VI does not refuse to countenance the idea or discuss it, he does not conceal his unfavourable attitude to it. In his letter to Cardinal Villot (2 February 1970), he wrote: 'Such a possibility calls for serious reservations on our part. Might it not be, among other things, a dangerous illusion to believe that such a change in the traditional discipline would, in practice, be limited to local cases of real and pressing need? Might there not be a temptation for others also to look on this as an easier solution to the current shortage of vocations?'

We need not go into the problem of clerical celibacy here. It is enough to indicate the drawbacks of the vast movement that seeks to get the churches of newly-Christianized areas to ordain married men to cope with the reduction in their numbers of priests. This movement seems to me to indicate too superficial an analysis both of the present crisis of the ministry and of what newly-established Christian communities actually need. I believe that the 'young churches' have not up to now worked hard enough to free themselves from the traditional patterns of recruiting and training clergy. It is obvious that the shortage of priests will be felt more intensely the more we seek to reproduce a Tridentine style of priesthood, adapted to a period, and to a religious and theological tradition that are not ours. In other words, it is not vocations that are lacking in the young churches—it is imagination: new Christian communities cannot be themselves unless they are prepared to work out new forms of church life, and abandon their unhealthy dependence on foreign personnel. And it seems to me that neither the ordination of full-time deacons nor yet the ordination of married priests is an original enough or bold enough solution.

It may be recalled that the Roman document on the ministry recognized certain functions for laypeople—functions which, at the time of the Council, appeared to call for the restoration of a full-time diaconate. For to be a lector was not merely to read the Scripture during mass—it involved several forms of service of the word; to be an acolyte might mean exercising the ministry of communion in liturgical assemblies where there was no priest. What, in such circumstances, would full-time deacons be? Super-laymen, or mini-priests? They certainly had no wish to be either; their position was quite difficult enough already, between a laity clamouring for more responsibility and a clergy accusing them of undermining their position. In point of fact, deacons are usually married men doing paid jobs. They would probably find it even harder to understand exactly where they fit in in terms of a redistribution of ministries, for it soon becomes apparent that there is no need to be ordained to the diaconate in order to fulfil the new functions in the community. Simon Tonye, Bishop of Douala in Cameroon, recently decided not to continue the experiment of married deacons begun by his predecessor. This is significant: the diaconate has the hallmark of a clerical institution. And indeed the introduction of the diaconate seems to have been thought up far too narrowly in relation to the shortage of clergy. Whereas, as Père Moingt points out, 'the needs of the faithful and of the Church in general are what should be our first priority. And what the Church needs today is to expand, multiply and diversify the channels of communication and responsibility within itself. The distribution of ministries must be considered from this point of view'.[8]

What we need, therefore, is a renewed understanding of the problem of ministries, taking as our starting point not the crisis of the clergy, but the situation and requirements of the various communities. It seems to me that any 'clerical' solution to the problem of ministries in the young churches is out of date and retrograde. Even the ordination of married men—for this apparently 'advanced' suggestion does not get at the root of the problem. Really, what should govern our approach to the problem of the Christian ministry, is a quest for autonomous communities.

In other words, in our churches, no Christian community has a future unless it can trust to its own inner dynamism, its continuing capacity to respond to whatever challenges it faces, its ability to develop its own resources and potential. Such a quest means a radical transformation of our ecclesiastical institutions, bearing as they do the impress of a clerical imperialism which has reduced the laity to the status of children and inhibited their power to act. In addition, if Christianity is to become incarnate in the life of a people, the community must be able to be fully autonomous in its form of organization. Hence, rather than laying down too many laws, each community should be left to work out its own course. This will call for a gigantic effort or decentralization. For, if we really want to see the faith expressed in people's own culture, the centres of decision must be implanted in the local communities. Thus, starting out from communities called upon to be responsible for themselves and self-sufficient, we must 'free' the Gospel, so that it can give rise to its own original conformations in each socio-cultural context. The problem of examining forms of ministry arises precisely in relation to those communities where there is no longer any rigid kind of organization imposed from above without roots in native traditions. In these conditions, surely we should re-think the relationship between the leadership of communities and the ministry of the sacraments, especially the eucharist. The question we must seriously ask is this: in the state of transition in which a young church finds itself, would it be contrary to the faith of the Church for whoever presides over the community, whose service is one recognized by the bishop—and in no way tied to the ordained ministry—to be empowered in some circumstances to celebrate the eucharist?

Could recognition of the ministry of presiding over a community not go together with a pastoral delegation to preside over the eucharist at which that community meets together and becomes a reality? Looked at in this way, would it not be proper to stress the 'official' character of a eucharist rather than the 'power' to exercise this particular ministry? The criterion for competence to carry out sacramental functions would then no longer be the laying-on of hands, but communion in the visible centre of unity in the local church. As long as the bond with the ministry of unity is maintained, the communion of the Church as a whole in the ministry of Christ in the Spirit would seem in such a case to justify a eucharist without a 'priest'.

Exploration along these lines is needed in the young churches today if the spiritual and pastoral needs of local communities are to be filled. It might not be necessary to wait for the Church to open new ways of access to the priesthood. The lack of an ordained ministry need not condemn the Church to decline. The fundamental problem faced by the young churches is that of 'localization'—a problem that ultimately stands or falls by the question of ministries. Neither a native clergy nor the massive presence of foreign missionaries constitutes a local church. It was thought that ordaining a native hierarchy represented the last stage in the 'implantation' of the Church in mission lands; but that is a clerical approach to the problem, part of the missiology of a legalistic ecclesiology. Since Vatican II, we have come to understand more clearly that 'a church is not truly established, does not lead a full life, is not a perfect sign of Christ among men, unless a laity worthy of the name exists and works along with the hierarchy . . . Hence, even in the very act of founding a church, great attention must be paid to establishing a mature Christian laity'.[9]

From this standpoint, when the Council insists that for local Churches to be worthy of the name, they must have 'ministers . . .

trained in good time and in a manner suited to the conditions of each Church'[10]; and one should not take the word 'minister' to relate solely to so-called priestly functions in the ritual sense of the term. Similarly, when we say that a particular Church should produce ministers from within itself, this must not be taken only to mean priests. According to the Council, 'from its very beginning, the Christian community must be so organized that, as far as possible, it can provide for its own needs'.[11] In fact, to organize communities so as to give the laity its place in the sum-total of ministries necessary to the development of the local churches would seem to be a valid answer to the problem we are discussing. In other words, rather than seeking at all costs to impose upon the young churches solutions that do not respond to their real yearnings or anxieties, we must leave the beaten tracks of traditional theology and explore new paths: we must *imagine* new solutions that are not just copies of the old ones—marked as these are by the historical relativity inherent in the shaping and conditioning of Christian life. Some really basic re-thinking, with a mind open to the questioning of the young Christian communities, can surely bring us out of the dead-end we have come to.

For in fact, the major problem for us is not the lack of ordained priests. We have somehow to bring the entire Church into the diaconate, in as much as every Christian is the deacon (or servant) of his brethren, in the image of Christ the servant of God and mankind. Taken to its logical conclusion, this would mean not so much ordaining people to the diaconate or priesthood, as developing the diaconal and priestly capacities of the Christian laity. The classic forms of institutional priesthood are no longer the answer to the basic problem of the ministry as it has existed in the Church since the hardening of the Counter-Reformation. The true ministry in the Church is the ministry of the people of God. What is needed, therefore, is to 'de-clericalize' ministries in order to give the laity access to the ministerial capacity of the Church itself. In short, what the young churches need, as do many others, is to use the ministries conferred by baptism.

The future of the churches depends on resolving this problem. If the young churches are to become autonomous, they must be 'localized' by being able to live on their own resources; this does not mean turning in upon themselves and rejecting all outside help, however non-alienating. What it means is that, in self-governing countries, the local churches too should be able to stand on their own feet. In a sense, admitting laypeople to various ministries is more than just a test of the young churches' maturity: it is also the necessary condition for any effort to implant and express the faith in the culture and language of the local people.

We must respond to the demands of our communities by making

fresh discoveries. There is no need to defend anything in our churches that is not moving towards new life. For our job is not to be guardians of the institutions of the Christian past, but to work for the future. And in this particular instance, it seems to me that nothing is fixed—everything remains still to do.

We must therefore discover fresh forms of ministry, letting ourselves be guided by the Spirit. There may be some ministries that should be restored; others, on the other hand, must come newly into being by a renewal of tradition (not to be confused with traditions). A reassessment of the laity, in the context of a renewed theology of the Spirit, will suggest to the young churches ways of resolving the problem of 'localizing' ministries. This new situation will stimulate in them a new self-awareness, given the right of local churches to explore and experiment which the Council specifically recognized. To manage with no priests, or very few, is a purifying ordeal, forcing the churches to make the most of the creative resources made available to them by the Spirit, in that margin for interrogation opened to the faith, so as to achieve a total interpretation of the Gospel for our time. The future will only be possible for our churches if they can free themselves of the institutions of the colonial churches and trust wholly to the creative initiative of communities in which men can become Christians, and serve both God and their own people: as St Paul put it, 'in whatever state each was called, there let him remain with God' (I Cor 7:24)

Translated by Rosemary Middleton

Notes

1. *Decree on the Missionary Activity of the Church*, chap. II, para. 15.
2. *Ibid.*, chap. IV, para. 23.
3. *Dogmatic Constitution on the Church*, chap. IV, para. 33.
4. *Ibid.*, para. 35.
5. *Ibid.*, para. 33.
6. Cf. Yves Congar, 'Ministères et Structuration de l'Eglise', in *Maison-Dieu*, no. 102 (1970), p. 18.
7. Cf. J. Moingt, 'Les ministères dans l'Eglise', in *Etudes*, September 1972, pp. 273–74.
8. Moingt, *art. cit.*, p. 291n.
9. *Decree on the Missionary Activity of the Church*, chap. III, para. 21.
10. *Ibid.*, para. 20.
11. *Ibid.*, Chap. II, para. 15.

Efoé Julien Pénoukou

Missionary Priests and the Future of the African Churches

IT may seem strange that one should still be talking about a subject that
has been covered in so many specialist journals, that has obsessed the
general chapters of missionary institutes, and may be painfully shock-
ing to many who have dedicated themselves with great generosity to
mission work. I would say with Père Congar that 'the difficult problems
we face today cnnot merely be dismissed as an attempt at subversion,
that things are not settled and established, and that there is still scope
for exploration'.[1] For no one can deny that today, traditional missionary work is undergoing a crisis of change, and there is still a need to
study all the circumstances and then explore ways and means of making that historic change successfully. My own modest contribution to
this sadly unimpassioned debate can be summed up under three heads:
to consider the various attitudes to the process of transition, to clear up
the ambiguity of a question that has been seen too subjectively, and
finally to state (though not resolve) the real problem, the future options
of the African churches.

FOREIGN MISSIONARIES: SHOULD THEY GO OR STAY?

When this question, be it real or imaginary, is put thus abruptly, it
produces differing and sometimes contradictory reactions. These may
be divided into four classes:

1. First there are those who envisage the closing-down of the missionary societies, their members voluntarily withdrawing in orderly
fashion. This is based on the view that the presence of a majority of
foreign missionaries in the churches of Africa is a brake on the
development of mature Christian communities. If the real powers of

decision, whether economic or ideological, are always in foreign hands, these churches will always be in the position of clients and subjects. What local Christians need is to be left to themselves, to take up their own responsibilities courageously, and so discover their identity and achieve autonomy.

This so-called radical position is accused of being 'contrary to the Gospel and the true teaching of the Church' in as much as it destroys the ties of Christian brotherhood, hinders cooperation between older and younger churches, and thus slows down the spread of the faith. It is also objected to, less fundamentally, on the grounds of being unrealistic; all the classic reasons are adduced—shortage of manpower, financial problems, and so on.

2. The ecumenical meetings in Bangkok (1973), Lusaka and Lausanne (1974) adopted a position not far from this: they proposed that the young churches should be brave enough to have a 'moratorium', or provisional break. For several years, they should manage without any foreign aid, and work with a free hand towards their own maturity; then, later, they should establish a relationship of equal collaboration with their mother-churches.

This proposal, which at the time came like a bombshell, was described by some observers as irresponsible. The idea of a 'moratorium' seemed to them to be an incitement to the young churches to a kind of autonomy of autarchy, of self-regard and self-sufficiency, whereas the Christian way towards responsible maturity should safeguard and improve the bonds of unity and mutual help with the universal Church. Possibly those who thus dismissed the idea of a 'moratorium' failed to understand its underlying purpose.

3. Another solution, the so-called moderate view, takes the precisely opposite line to the radical one, by affirming the need for missionaries to remain until the young churches can manage by themselves. Some people express this in more precise terms, suggesting that foreign missionaries be integrated into the local communities, as a living sign of the universality of the one true Church of Christ. The failings of the mission system must of course be remedied: pastoral techniques must be reviewed and renewed, the posts of greatest responsibility must be handed over, surviving remnants of spiritual colonialism abolished, and so on. In short, 'non-African missionaries must take into account the aspiration of the young churches for greater autonomy and more responsibility: they must make themselves available as needed, and take part in trying to build up Christian communities, under the leadership of the local hierarchy'.[2]

This gradualist hypothesis is also open to a series of criticisms. It is objected, in particular, that it represents an escape ahead of time by its refusal to confront the dangers of maturity. Furthermore, the numerical, economic and ideological security it defends rests upon a model of the Church and Christian society, a concept of the priest and his rôle, upon pastoral techniques and Christian praxis all of which were elaborated by other societies and to suit other times. This position, it may be urged, thus places the young churches inside a vicious circle, which both works from and tends towards a White ideal. The continuing presence of foreign missionaries will end by forming local Christians on the pattern of their former masters. Those who oppose such a solution also consider it a clear insult to the dignity and initiative of Africans, and an indication of lack of faith in the liberating and creative action of the Holy Spirit.

4. The attitude of the missionary societies fits in with the conception of a slow and phased transition. Their idea is to make themselves totally available to the bishops. The word 'service', as introduced at the Council and so popular ever since, is now used as a further justification for the missionary presence: 'we must offer the local churches the special service inherent in our vocation; we shall go wherever the bishops want us, wherever they want that special service . . .'[3] In the field however, there is a definite movement taking shape of migration towards the more 'underprivileged' dioceses, and the more recently-established bishops. In the missionary institutes, there is as yet no indication of any structural change at the top, though in terms of vocabulary and in matters of significant detail, real improvements are beginning to appear.

Those who oppose this attitude label it reformist; it is, they say, more concerned with the survival of the missionary societies than anything else, and conceals an unacknowledged wish to continue 'to be outposts of influence for their own countries, cultures and ideologies'. They see the dissatisfaction and sometimes even the deficiencies of the young churches as no more than the natural result of a missionary strategy of permeation. The missionary institutes, they say, are incapable of fundamental change, for they are essentially linked to the history which brought about the crisis of identity and survival from which Africa is suffering still.

The ever-sharper crystallization of attitudes relative to the going or staying of foreign missionaries in the young churches is disturbing, to say the least. It leads one to question the whole basis upon which the debate rests.

AN AMBIGUOUS QUESTION

The debate about traditional missionary activity, or rather about its future seems to me to start off on the wrong foot. On the part of the mis-

sionaries and some of the native priests, and even in the statements of
the African bishops, there is a tendency to state and interpret the problem in terms of personal aggression and negative demolition; or else to
'subjectivize' all the discussions, suggestions and criticisms that arise
around the existence of the missions. All attempts to resolve a problem
which is complex—to put it mildly—are too readily met with discouragement, confusion and anger.

But this is only because the question itself is so ambiguous—as well
as being asked rather late in the day, as though no foreign missionary
had ever before given a thought to preparing for his own departure. Yet
Cardinal Lavigerie wrote on 12 October 1874, in a directive to the
heads of seminaries, 'missionaries will primarily be the initiators, but
the lasting work will have to be done by the Africans themselves, once
they become Christians and apostles'.

Should foreign missionaries stay or go? The question is a false one,
because it misrepresents the point and meaning of the real question,
which goes far beyond the changes of mood or states of mind of a
particular group of men. In other words, such a question is only a real
question—in the sense of a quest for meaning and value—when it is
related to the formal and final cause of the missionary's working activity. Or one might put it this way: in the economy of salvation *in Christo,*
the work of evangelization is beyond the servants of the Gospel whom
the Master invites to work in his vineyard; as Scripture says: 'When
you have done all that is commanded you, say, "We are unworthy
servants" ' (Luke 17:10). It is therefore the problem of proclaiming the
Gospel—its necessity (I Cor 9:16), its content (II Cor 4:5), its purpose
(Titus 1:1)—that we have to pose first of all.

Consequently there is something rather specious about seeing the
future of the young churches as though considering the survival of a
corporation, in terms of the transfer of posts and responsibilities. Because, first of all, it does not stimulate local communities to effect any
rediscovery of the *fontes fidei.* Because it polarizes ideas and mobilizes
energies around what is secondary. Because it makes it impossible to
get away from subjectivism and authoritarianism, in other words to
liberate people's minds from the bitternesses of the past and open them
to the spiritual work of reconciling the world in Christ (II Cor 5:19). It
is as though the revelation of God and the sowing of his word in Africa
begin and end with the Missionary Institutes. Cardinal Daniélou would
have replied that it 'is accidental to Christianity that it has become
westernized'[4], and it is still accidental to the Christian churches of
Africa that they have received Christianity in a westernizing form. Nor
will it be essential to the content of their faith in the future to have an
Africanized Christianity. What matters, therefore, is to start from that
content—He who comes in the name of the Lord (Luke 13:36), Jesus

Christ, the supreme missionary—and keep going back to it.

But having said this, it would be mischievous to suggest that the staying or going of the foreign missionaries, and more important, their traditional concept and methods of evangelization, do not present a problem to the churches of Africa. The chain of reactions produced higher up is indication enough of a serious predicament. Nor is the problem, as some would have us think, one of re-examining the missionary consciousness of the universal Church (Mark 16:15). The discouragement and even disorientation spreading among missionaries, as well as the solution recommended (often quite violently) by the clergy and laity of the local churches—that they pack their bags and go. These, as well as the more deep-seated sense so many local Christians have of being torn between their traditional religious system and a missionary-style Christianity, are primarily social in nature, and relate to a history of foreign conquest and domination. But in the past few decades that history has moved into a new phase, with concomitant important social changes. The phenomenon of decolonization has brought about a new awareness among the young nations, and sharpened the confrontation between rich and poor countries. As the Asian bishops declared in Manila in November 1970, 'We are witnessing the awakening of the masses, and the end of their passive acceptance of poverty, ignorance, illness, injustice and exploitation . . .' It is no accident that whenever a military junta seizes power in any Third-World country, it uses the term 'revolution' to give it the stamp of legality. Furthermore, the taking over of positions of responsibility by the young churches is a reaffirmation of their determination to assert their own identity. Such a historical change—quite apart from the new ideas brought forward by the Second Vatican Council—inevitably brings the classic missionary situation into question.

In the West, indeed, the universal crisis is that of a world that is saturated, or rather, as Jean Lacroix describes it, of a society full of gaps and holes through which the very substance of the social body is escaping. And it is in precisely such a society that the crisis of missionary consciousness has come into being, even though 'in recent times missionary action has been functioning as an escape from the religious crisis in the West, a questionable shifting of the decisive problem posed by that crisis, and an effort to project its religious contradictions outside itself'. To recognize this and say it is not unkind or vindictive; it is merely an effort to clear up some of the ambiguity surrounding the question, so as to be able, as the ancient philosophers would say, to get to the reality behind appearances.

Then too, the fact that after a hundred years (on average) of evangelization, missionaries still represent the majority of the clergy in the young churches, casts a certain doubt on the way missionary activity works everywhere, and is in itself a source of uneasiness. The diocese of Yaoundé, for instance, with 535,000 inhabitants of whom 415,000 are baptized, has only 63 Cameroonian priests as compared with 110 missionaries; in Zaïre, for a Catholic population of over nine million, there are only 675 diocesan clergy, as against 2,500 foreign missionaries; in the diocese of Dakar, there are fifteen African priests and over a hundred missionaries; in Saint-Louis (Senegal), where the African bishop is from Ziguinchor, the 11 priests of the diocese are all missionaries—though it is true that of the 900,000 inhabitants, 99% are convinced Muslims, and there are in the town of Saint-Louis alone 59 mosques as against only two churches. But over all, we may say without fear of contradiction, that the young churches are more dependent numerically on missionary priests than on natives—which can hardly give either much cause for pride.

But, as I have said, that is not the root of the problem, any more than the question *whether* foreign missionaries should leave; what matters, rather, is to see *how* they could stay. And this question of *how*, which inevitably includes a fundamental reorientation of their attitudes and policies, is structurally bound up with the way the African churches see their own future.

THE CHOICE FOR THE FUTURE

The choice that lies before young Christian communities, and therefore also before all those committed to collaborating with them, is unique. It consists in setting on foot, now, a process of 'conversion', in the etymological sense, that will make it possible to take up the burden of colonial work everywhere, to shake off all the manifold ties of dependence on outsiders and above all, to give new life to the Christian culture they have received by infusing it with their own specifically African dynamic.

All this assumes that local Christian groups have been prepared to shoulder their own responsibilities, that traditional pastoral methods have been thoroughly overhauled, and that there has been a courageous critical look at a still far too clericalized Church. As a Malawian bishop, Mgr Kalibombe, wrote in a pastoral letter in 1973, 'the local church becomes alive and active to the extent that it becomes fundamentally self-sufficient both in its own inner life and its missionary obligations . . . to build a Church with the capacity to survive and grow even in the most critical conditions imaginable'. An act of faith indeed.

Such faith, a free gift from God, is also a fresh existential acceptance of the grace of salvation. The life of faith is more than just a reassuring 'deposit' that has been saved up over two thousand years: it must be for every people the coming of the incarnation of the Word of God. And for Africa, it must be a putting down of roots, a re-birth through the womb of its own socio-religious heritage as well as through a re-shaping of that heritage in accord with the radical newness of Christianity. There must be a total reassessment on the one hand of the cultural patrimony of black Africa, and on the other of the vocabulary and content of the 'theological superstructure' of the West which has for so long distracted us from the 'kerygmatic infrastructure'. African theologians, thank God, are already quietly working away, attentive to the voice of God, and determined to win the challenge of the future with all the poor in spirit. The future of a Christianity in which all men of good will, regardless of national or any other boundaries, will feel that they are sons of the same Father and brothers of the same Son, Jesus Christ.

In the human face of that Christianity, there will be neither white nor black, helper nor helped, missionary nor native; we shall all be one in Christ Jesus (Gal 3:26–8). Alas, this is still a long way off. So the debate on the future of the churches of Africa remains open, as well as on what the foreign missionaries ought to do. But I should like to make my own the wish expressed by J. Guéhenno: 'As one always leaves a margin on the written page, for revisions, corrections, things that may occur later, the truth one as yet can only hope to find, let us leave around our ideas a margin for fraternity'.[5]

Translated by Rosemary Middleton

Notes

1. *Au milieu des orages* (Paris, 1969), p. 57.

2. Cf. the Declaration of the Bishops of Africa and Madagascar who attended the Fourth World Synod of Bishops, *Doc. Cath.* no 1664 (17 November 1974), p. 995.

3. A. Laur, 'La mission des Pères Blancs', interview published by François Bernard, in *La Croix* (17 November 1974).

4. *Le mystère du salut des nations* (Paris, 1946), p. 52.

5. Congar, *op. cit.*, p. 56n.

Joachim N'Dayen

Relations of the Local Churches with Rome and the Function of the Episcopal Conference of Black Africa

SINCE 1969 it has pleased the Holy Spirit and the Holy Father to entrust me with the diocese of Bangui (Republic of Central Africa) and the administration of the diocese of Bambari where for six years one has been looking for a bishop.

This experience, although rather brief, has been long enough to allow me to evaluate—correctly, as I think—the relationship between the local churches on the one hand, and the function of the Episcopal Conference of Black Africa on the other. (For the moment I accept this last nomenclature.)

I have to admit, however, that it is not easy to put the matter of this relationship into writing, and this for various reasons of which I will explain some. First of all, the points with which our exchanges are concerned are manifold: ordinary pastoral work, specialized activities, ecclesiastical property, consultations about specific problems (usually without any danger to the changeability and perfectibility of solutions already laid down over there). It is difficult to tackle everything at once or even to provide a satisfactory global survey because the reality is so complex.

Then, it is not useless to realize that in the eternal city people are very touchy about these problems so that topics which are taboo can not be discussed without the whole discussion drifting into an atmosphere of pugilism. I have no intention whatever of plunging into fruitless controversy. But within the friendly circle of brotherly love in the

Church there is nevertheless room for the freedom of the children of God. I shall deal with the two themes mentioned above separately.

In the question of local churches I do not want to go back to the technical definitions which distinguish between 'local churches' and 'particular churches'. My confrère, Mgr B. Yago, archbishop of Abidjan, presented a paper on this at the Symposium of the African Bishops in Rome (1975, Report of the IVth General Assembly of SCEAM, pp. 94–104). I will rather refer to a certain 'praxis' which obtains between the two poles of our churches and the central direction from Rome, with all the ups and downs that mark the exchanges between people, even when inspired by the same ideal. Fr H. M. Legrand also dealt with the question in *Concilium*, no. 71, 'The Revalorization of the local churches: what is theologically involved?' (pp. 49–58).

It must also be pointed out that in so-called mission countries our constant relations are mainly with the Congregation for the Evangelization of the Peoples (Propaganda Fide). This Congregation acts as our liaison-officer between us and the other organs of Rome's government, so it seems. When, therefore, we talk about Rome, our contacts stop at that point so that it is very difficult for us to know whether our resolutions and our wishes penetrate beyond that screen. One admits that any bishop can meet the Holy Father for a fraternal exchange. Even Mgr Lefebvre, at the height of his rebellion, managed that! In 1969 a Synod had precisely to deal with the relations between Rome and the local churches. When, during the synodal sessions I listened to the speakers in that hall—very beautiful, indeed, but somewhat like a cellar—I had the impression that there was a communication problem between Rome and its ramifications throughout the continents. I have no means of knowing what went on before that date. The fact is that the bishops complained that a sort of hermeticism hampered the mutual relations. They reached the point where they wanted a more genuine practice of episcopal collegiality while maintaining the special condition of the charisma of the papacy. Since then, one has to say, we have been flooded with all kinds of papers, in spite of inflation.

I would now like to bring up the matter of our relations at both the *pastoral* and the *financial* levels, concentrating rather on the former than on the latter.

RELATIONS AT THE PASTORAL LEVEL

Every year the bishops have to produce a general survey of the state of the diocese: the progress of Christianity, the religious personnel, the parishes, the seminaries, the novitiates, ecumenical activity, catholic action, social communication, the liturgy. Every five years a more detailed report is expected. Finally, and in short, all pastoral activity has to pass through this process. And it is a good thing that the Roman bodies have a relatively clear idea of the local churches so that there is a kind of 'sympathy' with regard to the cause of the Gospel which the whole Church is responsible for. I have even been astonished to learn that these reports were read; that they were actually acknowledged, with attention drawn to one or other fact; that perhaps one might correct a bit more here and insist a bit more there.

Nevertheless, certain worries on our part found no echo or only met with a warning note. I'll give two instances.

Here is the first, and I'll put it very simply. In 1969 the regional Conference of the bishops of Central Africa and Cameroon had drawn up a motion in favour of a clergy which would include married men (initially laymen whose marriage had proved stable). This request was taken up again by the national Conference of the Central African Republic. I spoke to this motion at the 1971 Synod in Rome, and mentioned it again in an interview given to *Spiritus*. Thunder began to rumble down from the height of Olympus, and it became advisable to put these desiderata in low profile. Anyway, the Synod rejected the change by a small majority. Following the healthy practice of democracy, we put down our trumpets. We all did so, and I myself particularly, in an admirable act of faith.

Insofar as I am concerned, I accept that some ideas—even right ones—may be too inopportune and harmful to be put immediately into practice. And then strategic withdrawal becomes an act of virtue. The pope had also asked us not to get too excited about this point for the moment. The *status quo* would be maintained.

Here is the second example.

The episcopal conferences of the Congo and Central Africa had to consider a similar problem, almost at the same time: the matter of the possible admission to the sacraments of persons whose 'state is irregular'. After discussing the problem together, the bishops of the Congo were moved to pity by the fate of some faithful who were excluded from receiving the sacraments. They put two questions to Rome, worded as follows:

'Is it allowed to admit to the sacraments of penance and the eucharist a baptized man who is married by customary law, i.e., without the sacrament, and remains in that state because the partner refuses to go through a religious marriage, and when, for grave reasons, such a man cannot recover his freedom?

'Can one baptize a pagan woman, adequately instructed in the faith, but married by customary law as first wife to a baptized partner, and remaining in that state because, for grave reasons, she cannot abandon her husband?'

The reply showed no particular pastoral feeling.

'According to the norms in force, according to the contents of the letter of the Sacred Congregation for the Doctrine of the Faith of 11 April 1973, it is not possible to meet the "pastoral wish" expressed by the bishops of the Congo. It has rightly been pointed out that the two cases brought up are similar to the situation of the re-marriage of divorcees in western countries' (Letter to Card. Biayenda, Prot. 401, 29 June 1976).

The reply ends with a double barrage, perhaps salutary: 'ad utrumque: negative' ('No, to both questions'). Rejection all along the line.

Here, in the Central African Republic, we sent, as spokesmen for our faithful, a similar dossier to Rome. The Congregation began congratulating us on 'the attention . . . given to pastoral life" . . . It then said how pleased it was with the bishops for being so conscious of their duty to guide the clergy and the faithful and that usages which do not conform with the present discipline of the Church, such as the baptism of polygamists and the admission to the sacraments of persons who live in an irregular matrimonial situation, are carefully kept out of the pastoral ministry'.

One can imagine how proud we felt after all that praise. Then came our next question. We wanted to know 'whether the rigid attitude of the Church was dictated by profound and definite theological reasons or whether we were faced with a matter of simple ecclesiastical discipline?' (dossier CERCA, doc. 18, no. 10, p. 3). Don't be afraid: here is the reply: 'The general opinion is this: there is an analogy between the protest movements in Europe and those to which the document of the Central African Conference refers. Both Europe and Africa are dominated by two tendencies. The first is opposed to all structures, while the second advocates the priority of personal wishes and subjective needs over the established expression of the objective need. Now, because of its essential nature the Church is hierarchically constituted. It is therefore structured. Insofar as satisfying the subjective need is concerned, it has always had a subordinate place in the Church's practice, in accordance with that of our Lord himself in the Gospel, to the true, profound, objective need of the subject. The confusion between the subjective need and the objective one is the capital error of a physician. He should only consider the objective good of the sick person and not yield to his whim'.

I won't bother you with the rest. But one can only suppose that they thought we knew nothing about all that, although bishops of the holy Church, studious priests and pastors of souls, and endowed with the charisma of 'discerning the spirit'.

Nobody wants to upset the solid hierarchical structure of the Church, particularly not us, the bishops, who constitute the absolutely decisive elements of this structure. But our question was not about that.

Nobody wants to mix up the objective with the subjective. Yet, in all probability, subjective considerations have very likely saved a lot of people who are now seated at the right hand of the Lord. But it doesn't matter. Our question, which demanded a reply, at least part of a reply or an admission that at present it is impossible to give a decisive answer, still stands: 'Is the Church's rigid attitude dictated by profound and definite reasons or is it a matter of simple ecclesiastical discipline?'

Well, at the pastoral level this kind of communication is what we sometimes have to cope with. It is fascinating, and occasionally provides us with matter for our recreation.

RELATIONS AT THE FINANCIAL LEVEL

We can be brief about this part of the discussion.

At the time when our countries were occupied by foreigners (French, English, Portuguese, or what have you), the missionaries, supported by Rome, were also receiving aid from their respective countries, both from the Christians of the mother-country and from the states (the latter showing greater or lesser generosity according to their options with regard to the lay-oriented concept of their political system).

The missionaries themselves ingeniously tried to find on the spot the wherewithal to supplement what they received from abroad (bricks, soap, syrup, carpentry, coffee-plantations, etc.). They were most successful in this, often with a generous contribution by the Christians of the country. When the African countries became independent and the natives were given the total responsibility for their dioceses, there developed a certain disinvolvement of the Western states and their faithful in matters of economics. It therefore fell to the natives, bogged down in the rut created by their predecessors, to get out of this situation, but almost all still remain stuck with it.

This critical situation is rather effectively alleviated by some Catholic organizations. A fair number of them, however, will have nothing to do with the pastoral projects we are working out. They prefer us to rear pigs, as we have always done.

It is then that the moneys allocated by Rome are not only very useful to us but very often necessary. From this point of view the regular support given by Rome is comforting. But I am very much afraid that the suspension or deliberate diminution of these allocations are sometimes used as reprisals when bishops are deemed to be a little too difficult to handle. In fact, it seems to me that no bishop of the Third World has any interest in expressing highly personal ideas, however consistent with the church's tradition; the very fact that they come from the local churches which cling far more to the reality than the theories worked out elsewhere, means that the repercussions are felt in the annual income, particularly where the so-called 'extraordinary' requests are concerned. I spare the reader what I think are some striking examples.

On the other hand, better-known bishops and cardinals are admitted anywhere in Rome: those who have been more in the public eye at the Council or the Synod and those who can spend a little more time in Rome than in their diocese are rarely disappointed. And those who never express any embarrassing ideas always find a blanket when the weather gets colder; it is graciously offered by whoever has the power and it is sent directly from the banks of the Tiber to the docile addressee.

Another factor which, it seems, has a vast influence on those responsible for the distribution of the funds, is the place where the bishops have been trained. The 'ancient Romans' enjoy an enviable privilege. They drank the doctrinal milk at the sources of learning in the eternal city itself and possess a network of extremely interesting relations. But the others, the moujiks of the episcopate, were they not appointed by the Pope? Do they keep a more careful eye on the patrimony of their own relatives or on that of the local church?

Can one say that help is more forthcoming where there has been a personal attempt at self-financing? Having travelled a fair amount and carefully observed the situation, I would say not. I am rather reminded of the Scripture on this point: 'To those that have shall be given, and to those who don't have, even what they have will be taken away from them'. What I have said here does in no way diminish the admiration due to that vast organization which copes with distribution. I only wish it showed a little more sense of justice. Faced with this rapid survey of the relations between the local churches and Rome, and limited as it is to only two aspects, what is, in a general way, the function of the churches of black Africa?

THE FUNCTION OF THE CHURCHES OF BLACK AFRICA

Earlier on I mentioned the fact that one has to understand what is meant by the 'Episcopal Conference of Black Africa', because as such this organization does not exist.

What *does* exist is a continental re-grouping of episcopal conferences. The acronym SCEAM therefore stands for the symposium of the episcopal conferences of Africa and Madagascar. Its articles of association give it a structure which is supple enough to be less a

super-conference of national conferences than an association for discussion and united action.

I have to add that this symposium covers Africa and Madagascar and
cannot be limited to black Africa only. White Africa is part of it. I
therefore prefer the description 'symposium of the episcopal conferences of Africa and Madagascar' to the accepted one of 'conference of
the bishops of Black Africa'.

What, then, is the rôle which this association of episcopal conferences should play?

It seems to me that this symposium should be something different
from a kind of third order of I don't know what, which would always
move in the direction of a fixed, static tradition of the Church's institutions. On the other hand, if it must try to find its place within the
movement—which is life—it must evolve in the true tradition of the
Church. And that is the problem. It is not a specifically African problem. We share this worry with all the other bishops, and particularly
with the Holy Father, who heads the Church. This concern was excel-
lently reflected in the Synod of 1974. The symposium of the episcopal
conferences of Africa and Madagascar of 1975 continued this pastoral
concern. Pope Paul VI's address (26.10.75) once again formulated this
preoccupation which everybody shares. But I have to admit that I
agree with Mgr Matagrin, bishop of Grenoble, who, in 1971, more or
less said (I quote from memory) that when you drive a car in the mist,
your foot will be on the brake rather than on the accelerator. The
present state of the Church seems to be pervaded by this misty atmosphere. All the same, there is no need to despair that the mist will lift
and light will break through soon.

I would only bore all my readers by once again going through the
ideas that are current about the 'indigenization' of Christianity. Per-
sonally, I must admit that I have no firm ideas about that yet. I am
sitting on the fence between two attitudes: one favours the traditionalist
African (much more attached to old habits than is generally assumed)
and the other favours the African who wants to integrate the culture of
the African continent in the spirit of the Gospel.

The difficulties are legion. How can one impregnate Christian
thought with the whole of our own cosmogony, with the spiritual vision
of the Negro, without changing it fundamentally? How far should this
process of osmosis go proportionately? For it is certain that Jewish,
Greek and Latin ideas have profoundly influenced the presentation of
the divine message; the history of theology has shown this clearly
enough. It is in this sense that we, the symposium of the African
bishops' conferences, feel what we have to do while at the same time
being afraid of going beyond the normal limits of sound theology.

Taking the initiative, Rome is often ahead of us and hastens to stake out the direction in which it thinks we should go, out of fear that the blacks may pollute the teaching of Christ. The tendency towards syncretization is indeed prevalent in black Africa. It suffices to observe Kibanguism in Zaïre, and the prophetic Christianity of Zephirin which, starting from Pointe-Noire, is infiltrating Central Africa. Nor can one overlook the contortions and trances inspired by Haitian voodoo, which has definitely African roots.

And so, while everybody would like to see more liberalization of the dogmatic, moral and liturgical expression of Christianity, one is not very clear how to set about it—and I myself feel that way; one wonders how far one can go and still remain Christian. Since taking part in the great gatherings of the bishops of Africa, at synods as well as at the symposia, I can distinguish three main trends.

The first is rather inclined towards a certain immobility in religious matters, a certain complacent, cheerful conservatism, content with what exists and afraid of possible changes. A minority among the African bishops see themselves perhaps in that light. Then there is the group of those who have some inkling but prefer not to rush ahead. This makes them adopt an attitude of piously waiting for directives from Rome. This reminds me of a confrère who, at the Extraordinary Synod of 1969, vilified with incomparable zest the risky ideas stirred up in every direction by the western theologians, ideas which looked in every way like a fresh attempt at colonization. For him Rome was the life-buoy which saved him from being shipwrecked. This is the feeling of most African bishops.

Finally there is the group of *enfants terribles* of the churches on the African continent, thirsting for major changes, but changes for which they would like to have solid theological and scriptural foundations. But unfortunately, instead of these they produce almost nothing but anthropology and sociology, and this is not usually accepted as a decisive argument in the Church.

One can therefore assume that, whether at the national conferences or the regional ones or at the level of the symposium, the rôle of the African bishops is above all to become aware of what they are as a church; to know themselves fully, to take stock of all the human, cultural and spiritual available wealth, and to appraise it at its right value. It will then become a matter, not of adapting it all to the Gospel (too often taken as a kind of standard-weight), but of listening to how Jesus speaks in that context. Such an attitude demands first of all that one pray and meditate before setting the brain to work. After that the theologians and the other faithful, gripped by this vision—perhaps a new vision—express themselves, live and put something to the head of the Church which is not merely the fruit of cogitations during sleepless nights. And if all the African bishops tackled this together, honestly, in a Christian way if I may say so, it would be something very different from the present display of broken ranks.

I very much fear that this process is going to take a very long time. But then the Holy Spirit—who dwells in the bishops in a full manner—will not concern himself with our learned compositions on indigenous people and 'indigenization'.

Translated by Theo Weston

Gérard Eschbach

The Prospects For The Faith among African Youth

ONE way of seeing how the challenge of faith appears to that indicative sector, the youth of Africa, would be a descriptive analysis of the situation, a statistical report which would lead one to meditate more or less optimistically on the outcome, but this is not how I propose to tackle it. There are a number of such descriptions already in existence and because they do not go down to the underlying reasons they are incapable of leading to real understanding, let alone of suggesting courses of action that need to be undertaken. I prefer, at the risk of being mistaken, or of provoking some of my African brethren, to link my thoughts to an axis that seems to me essential. This is more of a hypothesis than a certainty and a hypothesis that is open to contradiction, but surely progressive truth has to be achieved through a process of dialectic, through facing and overcoming difficulties?

A DISTURBING DICHOTOMY

From the statistics alone it would seem that Christianity in Africa is in a happy situation: there is a spectacular growth in the numbers of the Christian community, a high level of religious practice, a plethora of vocations to the priesthood and the religious life. This impression seems to be confirmed on the spot: there is an abundance of associations, celebrations are fervently attended, the sacraments are well frequented, there is the conviction and commitment of a large number of believers and there are admirable examples of devotion.

There is then a multiplicity of favourable signs. Can one say there is vitality? Certainly. But whether there is a promise for the future is less certain because there are also less favourable signs. The most disturbing of these seems to me the dichotomy between faith and intelligence. This is a massive dichotomy seen at its most acute on the level of the lively intelligence of, and the culture represented by, thinking young people. One could of course say that this is a universal phenomenon today. One has only to look at the western nations. Yes indeed, but nevertheless the phenomenon does not seem to me to have the same meaning in the West as in Africa. Both its extent and its consequences seem to me qualititively different in the two cultural spheres, and far more serious in Africa than in the West. What is probably only growing pains in the latter runs the risk of becoming congenital malformation in the former.

If the West, faced with the challenge of the Gospel, shows disturbing signs of allergy, if its intellectual fashions are apparently far removed from the Gospel, it is nevertheless true that Western intelligence is still informed by a deep Judaeo-Christian reflex (perhaps one has to live for a long time in a different culture to begin to understand its extent and tenacity!) It is a sort of affect often more unconscious than conscious, historically and culturally determined by the great meeting between Athens and Jerusalem, a wrestle with the angel, the scars from which still mark the West in its onward march and even in its atheism and in its anti-Christianity, which still bear signs of the return of the prodigal son. There is a secret connivance between 'natural' intelligence and Christian intelligence which modifies the apparent dichotomy. Despite everything, there is a reciprocal challenge between the two and a fruitful confrontation is always possible.

In Africa there is nothing, or at least very little of all this. There it is as though the liveliest African intelligence functions in a radically different sphere from the Christian. Everything goes on as if Christianity had no part to play in the basic debates. It exists on the sidelines, with a powerful presence perhaps, but still on the sidelines. It gives the impression of having 'nothing to say' in both senses of the phrase: through the insignificance of what it has to say and through inattention to its relevance. Its presence and impact are marginalized by intelligence but powerfully taken up by the 'African religious soul'. The intellectual, if he still calls himself a Christian, is so in that part of himself that remains refractory to rational intelligence and which communicates with the powerful and obscure bio-sacral forces of cosmic and social ties. This part may be important but it is nonetheless something like an infectious disease. The dichotomy is lived existentially relegated to the mysterious zone of the 'religious', even if to a 'superior' form of the religious. Christianity is classified, pigeon-holed and defused. It can still have greater or lesser concessions made to it but it is no longer geared in with the dynamic of living thought and action.

The consequences of such a dichotomy in the immediate future and particularly in the longer term cannot but be alarming. There are three basic ones: *(a)* by hiding from a universal confrontation, the fact of being a Christian becomes of marginal relevance and concerned only with individual or collective subjectivity; *(b)* this marginalization tends to shut the Christian being off and risks making the Church a *sect*, which Larousse defines as 'a small group animated by a doctrinaire ideology'; *(c)* within this process there will then no longer be any barrier to a growing multiplication of more or less 'Christian' sects.

This is the fatal outcome once intelligence no longer challenges faith and faith no longer challenges intelligence. It leads to the establishment of two parellel orders whose power of attraction is very uneven: on one side there is the fascinating adventure of modern rationality blossoming in science, in technology, in ideologies of liberation; on the other there is a 'word' which one recognizes as beautiful indeed, and a brother-hood not lacking in warmth, no doubt, but belonging to the little world of the sacristy. How can an intelligent young African hesitate in choos-ing between them?

THE LACK OF A CHRISTIAN CHALLENGE

What future did the Christian faith have in men's eyes at its outset? One has to come back to this crucial question. History does not repeat itself but it does teach and one cannot fail to question the 'origin' (in both the diachronic and synchronic senses of the word) of faith in the different cultural spheres of the different fields of its mission in the light of history. When Paul preached the Gospel to the Graeco-Roman world he fully understood the part played by 'folly' in his preaching. Resis-tance did not come from the common people or even from the few eminent people who very quickly formed the first and admirable Chris-tian communities. Resistance came from the knowledgeable and philo-sophical intellectuals.

This factual situation could have given rise to a scenario in which the history of Christianity unfolded in this way: the different communities live their new faith with great fervour, giving free rein with almost dionysiac zeal to everything that religious emotion can intensify: mes-sianic utopias, charismatic rivalry, mystical ideology esoteric little groups . . . in short a burgeoning of diverse and varied 'sects' all based on a more or less consistent kernel of 'Christianity'.

Yet things did not turn out in this way. Why not? Essentially thanks to the establishment of a body of Christian thought. This was apostolic thought at first and particularly Pauline thought, then the Fathers, both Greek and Latin, and finally the immense theological work taken up and handed on from century to century. It was a Christian thought that both provoked and promoted culture—and yet the task was an unimaginable one. However scandalous the Gospel message, it at least germinated and took root in the mental and cultural sphere of Semitism and Judaism. The original Mission then inevitably forced the meeting between this Judaeo-Christian mental and cultural sphere and the Indo-European-Greek mental and cultural sphere. Two spheres which could not possibly be further apart: Athens and Jerusalem: a whole series of radical paradoxes: being or creation; logic or liberty; immanence or transcendence; transcendence-flight or incarnation; eternal return or history; finite or infinite; fate or destiny; immortality or resurrection; fault or sin; steady pace or leap forward; Eros or Agape. . . . a formidable reciprocal challenge and one taken up again and again by both sides. Even in this modern age the West has not ceased, consciously or unconsciously, to live culturally on the basis of this vast challenge constantly posed and constantly renewed, which constitutes the dynamic kernel of its inner dialectic.

This over-rapid recourse to history throws up three important points: (a) Christian questioning does not merely not pass by the living questioning of a whole culture but confronts it as its challenge, provokes it and forces it forward; (b) thanks to this vitality of Christian thought the Gospel, far from crumbling into sects, has been able to constitute itself in a Church; (c) this original experience with regard to one particular culture, an experience which has remained living throughout the course of this culture, will polarize Christian thought to the point of rendering it less able to undertake the same task in relation to other cultures and to all cultures. Now Christianity came to Africa through its Western incarnation. It could not have been otherwise. Africa was immediately accessible to, and permeable by, not only Christian faith but the Western incarnation of this faith. Too easily accessible, one can say, for there not to have been some misunderstanding.

One disturbing fact stands out amongst the others: it is a terrible thing to say, but there is no heresy in Africa! (When one thinks of the dynamic challenge that heresy has always provided in moving thought forward!) In Africa there have "only" been slidings away, signs of secret and informal resistance movements—which probably go very deep all the same. In any case they are infinitely more disquietening than explicit 'heresy'. A true confrontation has not yet taken place. Without doubt it will—in fact it must! This in the logic of the incarnation. The outlook for the faith in Africa depends on the outcome of such a confrontation through which an authentically African-Christian thought and theology in the widest and strongest sense of the word will be achieved, an embrace (a loving embrace under the sign of *Eros* and of *Thanatos*) between the authentic word of God and the authentic word of man—of African man.

This, I believe, is the point at which the thousand and one particular difficulties come together and from which the outcome for the future of faith amongst intelligent young Africans will develop. It means breaking the tragic circle where effect plays cause and cause becomes effect.

If we have here put our finger on the central knot of difficulties we must now try to discover reasons for them and to analyze the epistemological and pragmatic obstacles standing in the way of development. The phenomenon will only become comprehensible on the level of these reasons and only then will effective action become possible. Having reached this point I must confess to a certain anxiety. The rest of what I have to say would require long analysis: it is only on the basis of a constantly renewed and constantly varied experience through a thousand particular events that reflection can lead to a convergence of ideas. So how in the short space of an article can I demonstrate the multiform complexity of these reasons without betraying their coherence? One would need more space than is available to describe the particular events themselves on which the reasons are based. Lacking this space, I will have to be content with a somewhat dry enumeration of schematic propositions.

CIRCUMSTANTIAL REASONS

These are the external reasons, those immediately apparent, situated on the conscious level and explicable in speech. They are therefore the easiest ones to deal with, which does not mean that they are lacking in strength and tenacity.

(*a*) The historical moment of the meeting between Africa and the Gospel is unbelievably more 'encumbered' (ideologically, politically, economically and technologically) than was that of the meeting between the West itself and the Gospel. The relevancy of the Good News is therefore drowned in the midst of a host of relevancies.

(*b*) Christianity came to Africa through its Western incarnation and has not succeeded in working the necessary release from this Western orientation. There is a sort of original sin at the historical origin of faith.

(*c*) Contrary to the case in the meeting between Judeo-Christian culture and Graeco-Roman culture, in the meeting between the West and Africa it was the culture rich in 'possessions' (technological, scientific, and so on,) and strong in 'domination' that brought the Gospel. The terrible ambiguity stemming from this is that the Gospel is seen as compromised with an 'imperialism'.

(*d*) The West which (also) brought the Gospel is a constant and effective witness to values that go directly against those of the Gospel. This is a living contradiction that can only reduce the importance of the Christian message in African eyes. What, in particular, can one say of the scandalous compromise of a West regarded as Christian with the injustice of an economic world order that upholds and even aggravates underdevelopment?

(e) Together with the Gospel, the West is giving Africa critical weapons for fighting the Gospel and ideologies that negate the Gospel.

(f) Through a reaction against ancestral religiosity on one hand and through the seduction of new models borne along by modernity on the other, salvation in Jesus Christ is not only diminished in appeal but suspect.

(g) To the extent that it is (still) significant, the Christian message is made part of the 'religious' sphere. It belongs almost exclusively to the cloistered sphere of pietism and of an anti-intellectualism.

(h) At the same time there is a powerful assertion of a 'humanist' ethos, showing a naive pre-critical optimism in regard to human possibilities—very eighteenth-century style.

(i) But it is still disconcerting, given the lack of identical historico-cultural reference points, to see how virulent is the questioning of modernity, in which the very ground of the question is submitted to a more and more generalized relativity, and where, far from being given in an absolute manner, replies have to be found in the future climate that will emerge from a dialectical leap forward.

(j) The ever-increasing pace of historical progress works in the same way. Languages in a world in rapid evolution not only vary but multiply. The future is then as it were telescoped and intelligence inevitably goes through a moment of inertia before it can take off.

(k) Of course, the meeting between conflicting viewpoints is itself fruitful in the ambivalence of challenge or alienation, but because the meeting between Africa and the West has come from a unique relationship between dominant and dominated, Africa has been unable to benefit from it as from a promoting challenge and has continued to resent it as an alienation.

(l) If intelligence needs difference it equally needs identity. Identity integrates difference and difference leads identity forward dialectically. Now, the African mind has been too harshly plunged into too much difference. The West still has the greatest difficulty in finding its feet in the difference it is continually engendering, while Africa, still traumatized by the colonial experience, is inevitably going through a crisis of identity.

(m) The sharp assertions of identity and authenticity coincide precisely with the awakening of nationalism. This leaves the Churches socio-politically placed between compromise and the latent but none the less explicit menace of something like a *Kulturkampf*.

(n) His recent colonial past and present state of underdevelopment give the young African an acute feeling of frustration, which is shared in solidarity and expresses itself in self-assertion. It is not in Christianity but in Marxism that he seems to find the ideology capable of integrating this frustration and this assertion into coherence, one that can take his nationalism into Third World solidarity and give him an effective weapon with which to struggle.

(o) The 'progressive' ticket is enormously seductive for young Africans. It is therefore 'smart' to profess atheism, which is seldom the fruit of intellectual reflection but sometimes a weapon of militancy and more often an alibi for a 'materialistic' frenzy of desire for the consumer goods of the modern world.

(p) Yet deep down, the African is generally resistant to atheism. True atheism is only really possible (in the final analysis) on the basis of Christianity. Now Christianity has not (yet) succeeded in truly penetrating the African mind. This has lead to a pseudo-atheistic flourishing of neo-divinities (with their symptomatic capital letters: Science, Nature, Progress, State, Party, Leader, etc., etc.,) since there are too many possible patron saints to choose from.

All these reasons, and all the possible combinations of different ones, go some way to explain why the African mind has reservations about Christianity. These reservations, however, are generally less in evidence as structured and explicit thought than as an intellectual and pragmatic 'climate'. The dichotomy and the lack of challenge we spoke of earlier are in evidence here. There is a sort of generalized diffuse indifference covering the whole middle ground between exceptional hostility and outright sympathy. The basic question is really whether Christianity comes into the question at all.

Underlying all these circumstantial reasons there must then be far deeper reasons affecting the mental and cultural climate in which the relationship between 'Africanity' and Christianity is played out—the difficulties of Christianity in regard to Africanity: the obstacles placed by Africanity in the way of Christianity. Here the ground is even more shifting and the approach to it therefore still more hypothetical.

ARCHAEOLOGICAL REASONS

The term means that these reasons underlie the others. They are sub-soil from which the roots of the tree draw their sustenance. They lend themselves only indirectly to clear understanding and can only be uncovered by a searching 'outside' examination.

(a) There is the paradox of two mental outlooks with a completely different polarization: the biblical outlook is more geared to the millennium, the African to utopia. So there is a conflict between the risk-taking adventure and the search for security; between fatherly activity and return to the maternal bosom; between the conquest of the Kingdom that is to come and installation in an earthly paradise; between revolutionary excess and institutional harmony; between historical urgency and a self-repeating inactivity; between the doubts of faith and the wisdom of gnosis.

(b) The African mental climate is widely affected by an ontological tropism. Being is; not being is not. Deeply felt, this as it were spherical and harmonious fulness of being underlies what the West is more and more beginning to envy Africa; its intensity of communion, depth of community bond, power of participation, fulness of presence, wisdom of knowing how far to go—a sort of immense ontological optimism.

(c) In such a mental and cultural climate, values of constitution and therefore of security, logically take precedence over values of adventure and risk. The functional becomes more important than the relational, the sum than the part, the relative than relativity, being than 'ought to be', consumption than production, acquisition than the tool, arrangement than revolution, religion than faith.

(d) At the same time, anything that can weaken the logic of this ontological tropism risks being excluded: time as irreversible and heterogeneous becoming; history as revolutionary urgency; production of radical novelty; the far horizons of personal destiny; the anxiety of long-term planning; the importance of the "here and now" as grace or sin; openness to the future.

(e) As the ransom of this ontological optimism stands the great objection: if God exists, why do we not possess everything, why do we not know everything, why does man have to go on working, creating, seeking?

(f) Being is being-with: as sons of the same mother, African individualities seem only to find themselves in the bosom of their community. Personal freedom is suspect and there are a thousand defence mechanisms operating against it. This creates admirable organic solidarities but at the same time risks stagnation through lack of confrontation. The African Churches are afraid of prophets.

(g) The predominance of lunar archetypes over solar archetypes, which corresponds to an atrophy of the super-ego, allows African man to spare his 'unhappy conscience' and live in more immediate communion with the fulness of life. This weakens his sense of sin, of responsibility and of transcendence.

(h) Being is, life is, man is, in plenitude and with no other reference than to that-which-is. Without a bad conscience and without metaphysical anxiety, this is the integral humanism of man as the measure of all things, even of space and time. To the detriment of the set square, plumb line and clock—even of categories of understanding.

(i) This integral humanism doubles with a sort of existential structuralism. Far from being a polemical challenge, stimulating novelty, contradiction tends toward a form of integration that reduces tension to the minimum. Hence an incredible capacity for compromise: doesn't everything always work out?

(j) The vicissitudes of dialectic in Africa: if being is fulness, negation can only be non-being—absolute. Being absolute, negation can in no way contribute to promotion of being. The third dialectical term (which implies a transcendence) is excluded. Dialectic tends to be reduced to a coming and going or to negation: what cannot be overcome can only be denied. At this level Marxism fares no better than Christianity.

(k) The result is that difference, far from promoting new thought and action, far from being a dialectical challenge, risks being seen either as an obstacle to be avoided (rejection), or as a model to be imitated (mimetism), or as a contribution to be picked over and salvaged (eclecticism).

(l) In Africa the Word is more dialogue than dialectic, more communion in fulness of meaning than confrontation of critical reasoning, more unequivocal statement than discovery in the midst of equivocation. Hence the difficulty of talking about God, which is always inevitably false and yet true at the same time. Hence the difficulty of progressing beyond a literal reading of the Bible and the difficulty of reading the progress of faith through history.

(m) Given this radical ontological optimism and this integral humanism, what need can there be for salvation in Jesus Christ—concretely or existentially? This is a question that African theology has not yet succeeded in facing.

(n) In such a mental climate the most serious problems are perhaps posed, in what concerns Christianity, by the reality of transcendence—not the non-Christian transcendence-flight but transcendence-incarnation: that being, that life, that man should be open to a radical possibility of change going beyond a possible break; that man should 'infinitely surpass man'; that God should be at once with us and at the same time 'totally other'. The verticality of the act of faith in contrast to the integral sphere of the 'religious'; the extremism of the possible impossible; the immoderation of sin and of grace; the infinity of human freedom. The incarnation: God become man so that man can become God. The creation: there is no destiny—

everything including being and nature is open to creative freedom. The resurrection: everything can be taken up at every moment into a radical novelty. The parousia: history is not fatality but meeting in a going beyond. The redemption: there is no such thing as an absolute negativity; everything can be grace.

As I said at the beginning, the question is more important than a hastily thought-out reply. The question is an agonizing one, but would be infinitely more so if at least a certain number of young Africans were not asking it for themselves. Happily they are, because once one starts seeking everything becomes possible and if this analysis provokes more thought then the outlook is happier still because research is only possible through provocation. Is God not the 'Other' who continually challenges and pushes us? We have to believe in the opportunities brought by every meeting of differences, and the greater the differences the greater the opportunities. Can we not see the time coming when Africa will finally dare to provoke the theology that is still too marked by Western regionalism?

Translated by Paul Burns

Anselme Titianma Sanon

The New Gospel in a Millenarian Church

CAN evangelization help renewal? Does the Catholic Church in Africa have a future? On what conditions? What demands have to be fulfilled if this future is to be an African development of the Church and an ecclesial evolution for Africa?

The questions dissolve into a devout wish that the bi-millenarian Church should become the true Catholic Church in Africa without traducing the legitimate aspirations of an Africa confronted with problems of authenticity and cultural identity. Surely the Catholicity which in principle can only grow richer through this African dimension runs the risk of trying to control Africanism, or of rejecting it on being rejected by it.

How is a two-thousand-year-old body to rediscover its youth in the joy and pain of bringing new and young churches into the world? How is it to be born again?

The objection which was contemporary with Jesus and posed by Nicodemus, is something we often remember painfully in many African Christian communities.

As far as I am concerned at present, it is not necessary to proclaim Africanism or Africanization, which have enough defenders and justifications. Instead it is time once again to address my Catholic awareness to the evolution of the Catholic Church on African soil. As in the apostolic experience of St Paul, the trials emanating from our brothers threaten more obstacles for us than those that usually come from without (2 Cor. 7:5; 11:26–29). In order to assess the possibilities of the situation and the risks of Christian and African renewal, I shall raise the question of the interconnections of the confrontation of the Gospel with African culture in terms of the demands of the Gospel. For the first Christians (as in our own communities in the first century of their history), baptism and therefore the Gospel introduced a new world. But will the testimony of the Church now be received in such a way that the young churches become the yeast of evangelical renewal in the life and history of their nations on the one hand, and in the bi-millenarian advance of the Church as a whole on the other hand?

That would mean that our witness was recognized both by our cultural worlds and by the universal Church, and that we also are the Church (Acts 10:15–18; 11:1 ff.), for the Gospel also belongs to us (Acts 2:39; Eph. 2:13–17). In order to grasp the ecclesial implications of this situation in its theological dimension, I shall start with the relations of the African Church with its original cultural world, as well as the novelty of its original church witness in the Catholic family, the universal Church.

THE IMPACT OF EVANGELIZATION ON AFRICAN CULTURES

I shall start with the original environment of the Christian communities. When we realize that one third of the total population of Africa is Christianized, it is permissible to ask whether the Christian faith introduced any truly dynamic process into the African cultures. If the answer is Yes, we have to know if that process is injurious to the millenarian aspect of the Church, and to the African cultures. This gives rise to a greater problem: the cultural effectiveness of the Gospel in general, and its impact on African cultures in particular.

How was the gospel message received in Africa? In many areas the first evangelization and the first conversions produced generations of Christians charged with the responsibility of being the Church in their socio-cultural environment.

Obviously the actual introduction of Christianity which gave rise to these young communities encountered cultures, mentalities and traditions which resisted the influx and expressed their reaction in negative or positive attitudes which touched on the radical essence of church witness.[1]

The cultural introduction of Christianity in its doctrinal aspect (orthodoxy and orthopractice) was a novelty for the religious awareness of many Africans whose religious customs were often much less successfully constituted and formulated.

The doctrinal statements of the Church, above all when they did not turn dogmatic formulations into very simple formulas, did not seriously disturb the underlying African mentality.

The communication of the message was often carried out in terms that were culturally alien and unusual, and therefore without roots and any dynamic cultural support. The doctrinal assimilation which is still in process often escapes any fundamental questioning. Admittedly confrontation between what one learns and what one knows about one's ancestral past occurs here and there, mainly in the area of ethics, but communication and assimilation are still weak as a result of the didactic and methodological poverty of the instruction given.

The few reactions observed show either a total rejection of given Christianity, or a questioning that represents the attitude of young disciples. Some people ask questions in order to understand, in order to know if they have reacted to the right degree in order to be affected by the matter, not in order to put forward radical objections.

That is why no Christian apologetics has arisen from the confrontation between African thinking and the African world, and the Gospel. Nor has there been a sufficiently consistent development in regard to the profound expectations of culture. Hence the catechism was presented as if to an unbelieving, indifferent or even hostile environment, to the extent that atheism and rationalism were self-produced by that very catechesis. However, I shall mention three points where interfertilization between the Gospel and African tradition is promising.

1. The first includes all communication problems. There is of course no Christian faith except when the Christian faith is transmitted and received.

I am aware of the catechetical problems linked with the methods of transmission of the message, and therefore I ask what has to be transmitted and how it should be received. The doctrinal development of the western Church in certain ages gave an impression that the intellectual reaction to the message offered a guarantee where intelligent comprehension and grasp were most important. Those who are surprised that peasants or illiterates have a deeper grasp of the faith than intellectuals reveal their inadequate understanding of the faith.

The fact that the good news has to be transmitted so that it is understood and grasped, implies (among other things):

—that the recipient understands the content before any explanation is given;

—that he should feel affected and concerned;

—that he should feel understood: that is, that whatever objection he is able to express, and whatever doubts and anxieties, should find illumination within his new faith.

It seems normal that the recipient of the message given in this way should feel received and accepted by its bearer, and that a relationship or communion should come into being between the messenger and his disciple: that is, the actual birth of the church in the Church.

Among the problems raised, the following deserve to be noted: the fact that illiterates have to be evangelized. Several techniques are available to the preacher for catechesis of illiterates. Instruction in literacy can be used as an instrument of evangelization, or the illiterate can be met on his own ground by recourse to oral tradition; then the catechist has to learn a language. But that implies a style of transmission of the message which relativizes the academic and compelling nature of Scripture. Hence we have to rediscover an oral form of instruction which is alien to the approach of Scripture. It is the method by which a group learns by heart, not the method addressed to isolated individuals.

Then the Scripture resumes its dimension as Word, for the Bible is the Word of God: it is only partial in its written form, for tradition as a whole consists of gestures and words in intimate union.[2]

LITURGY AND SACRAMENTS

As a whole, the Christian liturgy, even after Vatican II, has been far from satisfactory for our Christian communities.

What is missing from the present liturgy is experience, which has been replaced by a much easier ritualism that uses words and things in a dimension that avoids their profound symbolism.

But in an experiential grasp of the world, and therefore of the liturgical act which is a translation of that encounter, the real becomes more than it is; the real is the link between what is; it is not just what seems to be, or declares itself by the evidence of the senses, but what is happening behind the veil of signs. The real is to some extent sacramental. Any rejection of this dimension makes the liturgy and sacraments rather dull and vague. It is too strong to say that people prefer the stations of the cross or a baptismal ceremony to a mass, because popular religiosity and social solidarity are factors here. It is more appropriate to take into account the experiential power which is missing from many masses where the Eucharist is 'manufactured' by a process of rites and formulas approved by the competent authority. Here too the discovery of the liturgy and the sacrament by the intermediary of symbolism and experience is a major factor of African Christianity. The African sects are well aware of this, and the appropriate development of the liturgy is a major aspect of the future of the African Church.

THE FAMILY AND COMMUNITY DIMENSION

In many young communities, there seemed to be no term for the Church. Here and there the rejection of the Latin, French or even Greek term resulted in the image of the great assembly or the sacred assembly. How is that to be translated without omitting the images of bodies and people, of assembly and unity?

The image of the great African family seems to be emerging progressively. More than one theologian equipped with an 'African sociology' would be able to discern and denounce its ambiguities. But here African experience is able to make us rediscover the typological dimension of a symbol, in the sense that the symbol, by uniting opposites, elicits a more profound understanding of the underlying reality, while purifying the social or sociological reality drawn on.

The great African family, in spite of its gerontocratic deficiencies and its hazy limits, allows the values of collective solidarity to be grasped together with those of familial fraternity, of human community in a whole to which one belongs through birth, alliance and affinity.

THE RELIGIOUS POLITICS OF A CHURCH LOOKING FOR ACCEPTANCE

On what conditions will the Church be accepted by African cultures? Without engaging in prophecy, I shall give some indications.

The impact of the millenarian Church will only have a new salvific effect on African cultures if it acts in humble *kenosis*.

The Gospel, in source and transmission, has a cultural dimension; it acknowledges cultural autonomy, and respects its own existential reference.

As human adaptation to reality, culture in all its diversity includes human behaviour on a basis of mind and local knowledge. The Gospel, in respecting cultures, also respects the autonomy of types of moral wisdom which support that human behaviour. It receives them charitably and stimulates them to act according to their own genius, while at the same time purifying them.

Of course dialogue is the first justification for this attitude of respect. But more deeply, cultural autonomy has to do with redemptive creation. Throughout his earthly condition, man has been searching (Acts 17:17) to rejoin God, by virtue of the capacity that God gave him. It is characteristic of man to respond to God's attempt to bring men to worship him in spirit and in truth (Jn 4:23), as in religion.

By revealing this vocation, the Church should be able to help the rise of new churches in African cultures, on the basis of their religion and wisdom. If we admit that the evangelization of Africa produces original Christian communities, a vital question arises: are the millenarian Church and the African world receiving their testimony?

An understanding of the relations of the African churches with the greater Church and their original ground will enable us to rediscover the points on which relations between the local church and the preceding Churches centre.

THE AFRICAN CHURCH IN THE MILLENARIAN CHURCH

Are African churches being born and do they have a right to exist? These banal questions raise problems connected with ideas and visions of the Church and of independent churches. I shall reduce these ideas to three which underlie recent pastoral attitudes.

The pastoral vision of Christianity is the most familiar in the Church. From its centre outwards, the Church tries to assimilate new areas: the mission countries. The person for whom the Gospel is intended in those foreign parts is the 'foreigner' (hence foreign missions) merely because he is located beyond the limits of the Christian zone. Overwhelmed by this strong current from the central spring, or hidden in the forest where it is implanted, the young churches are never able to rejoice in their youth. They will soon be treated as subsidiary churches, taken into the bosom of the great family of the Church. Equipped with expatriate structures and architectures, they will have no leisure for original experimentation. Ultimately they may stagnate, as do churches unaware of the serious aspect of their existence. Their efforts to find an original means of expression will meet with an amused or suspicious reception, or one that is inquisitive or too flattering.

Thanks to impulses from the gospel of secularism, missionary evangelization occurs in the action of a Church which renounces a worldly—even a Christian worldly—existence in order to recover its spiritual distance and its responsibility in relation to it.

The Church enters nowadays into a world of increasing pluralism. The identity of this world which cares so much about its identity is not without effect on the styles of a Church more than ever in a state of tension in regard to its internal unity and identity. The faith of this Church will no longer be a covering for a world given once and forever. It must be the thread which enables the various elements of a multicoloured tapestry to be assembled. Because of this bias the face of the Church will mould the face of the world, and *vice versa*.

If we acknowledge the spiritual break and cultural grounding which characterizes the Church in its relation to the world, we have to admit that the Church cannot be the Church unless it is that sort of Church in this kind of world. Certainly the affirmation of humble and joyous assurance in *Lumen Gentium* 8 seems more authentic. The Church, as Christ wanted it, subsists essentially in the Catholic Church.

But the Church of Jesus Christ, like the United Nations Organization peacekeeping on jealously guarded frontiers, is surely no more than a juxtapositioning of churches which enjoy charitable connections but perhaps not firm structures. The diversity and identity of the young churches on the cultural and spiritual level should provoke the universal Church into showing new courage. It is not enough for the greater Church to state that it subsists in different ways in the various church communities coming to birth: it is necessary for those communities and for itself that those communities should be recognized as truly the Church.

AN EVANGELICAL PASTORAL

The dead-ends reached in our time by the system of missionary expansionism that has operated since the foundation of the Congregation for the Evangelization of the Nations indicate the end of a system. Something has changed which should change other things in the evangelizing Church as well as in the evangelized world.

The missionary departure from the centre of the Church to the peripheries was seen as a contagious spread; it would establish the faith by establishing a church or churches. A misunderstanding of this growth (which is not an expansion, but a form of autogenesis), has given rise to the unfortunate impression of a Church with rigid central structures attempting to promote similar structures in far-off lands.

The problem of missionary adaptation raised by a few theologians or liturgists is the outward sign of a real misunderstanding about what the Church is, and about its mission of evangelization. The decree *Ad Gentes,* which is praiseworthy for its openness in certain passages (for instance no. 2, where it is stated that everything should be submitted to a new scrutiny), depends as far as the first few paragraphs are concerned on this mentality. The pastoral on Missionary Evangelization is directed to the self-renewal of the Church: the permanent genesis which occurs when the Word brings together believers to revive the apostolic experience (Acts 2:42).

THE AFRICAN CHURCH IN AFRICAN CULTURES

The African world allows the Gospel a certain receptivity which arises mainly from traditional milieus but also from modern Africa. Relations between the African Church and these milieus imply three areas of dialogue; with the régimes, with Islam, and with ideas and ideologies: that is, with politico-cultural evolution.

The response of our communities can only reach its full dimension if certain facts are explained: such as the cultural existence of Christ, and of the Gospel and of faith in the Church. Until now these data have often remained in an implicit state—until, that is, the appearance of the African churches. Their primary claim is their legitimate right to be the church within the greater Church. The second is: to enjoy an authentic relationship with their own socio-cultural world. In fact an authentic African church ought to be a force for innovation and creativity in African culture. Then there is a radical choice (this is no question of efforts in favour of a specific culture, but of the very future of the Church): In Africa as elsewhere, the Church cannot be a church outside the world. This cultural dimension, which accompanies every instance of the Church, makes possible a variety of styles.[3]

In fact, if Christianity were only a western phenomenon, we young communities would be no more than export products; but where Christianity has left its Mediterranean birthplace and has passed beyond the frontiers of the Mediterranean and western world, it is fulfilling its catholic vocation and showing itself to be capable of a universally applicable human culture.

Aware of that, the Church as a whole should revise its dogmatico-theological definition of its own identity, of what it actually is. If the Church presides over the great community of love, it is only right that it should know who is summoned to this assembly and what exactly is the constitution governing membership. In other words, are the local churches mini-churches or true churches in their own right?

If the answer is Yes, then the Church should now learn how to express its real image, the true identity showing forth its essential nature, in regard to the nations of the world and in regard to its ecclesial evolution in all those nations. Of course, it has done so in the past. Why should that dynamic power and capacity be exhausted in the future?

During recent socio-political changes which have marked world development, such as colonization and colonialism, independence movements and under-development, negritude and authenticity, or even the Movement for African Unity, the authenticity of the vocation of the Christian Church has been put to the test.

It was a matter for the Christian consciousness to express the authenticity of its mission in relation to these movements and ideologies. In fact it proved difficult to affirm the Church's solidarity, or rather that of its members, with the fate dealt out to these countries. Certainly the fear of too great political involvement in ambiguous situations has played a role in this tendency. But it is above all an inability to express the spiritual core of the Gospel message which has really been at fault. What significance could it have for our situations?

To win credibility, the African churches have to demonstrate the identity of their essence as churches in relation to their cultural authenticity. They have to be the Church and to be it without disloyalty to their African dimension. That demands as prerequisites their deep commitment to the Gospel in the Church and their roots in local cultures. The desired situation is one in which the Gospel recovers its value as news of resurrection and revolution.

NEW EVALUATIONS

The arrival on the scene of the new churches is an invitation to the greater Church to rethink its real way of life and to re-evaluate former options which might well be less meaningful today. Whether they are growing old or not, the founding churches are old in the eyes of the young, growing churches. Yet these young churches cannot lay claim to true originality unless certain questions are first answered. Some of them are: the meaning of the mission of evangelization; the translation of the Gospel; and, finally, the faithful response of the evangelized.

In its missionary consciousness, the Church has to cross certain geographical, physical, cultural, sociological and psychological frontiers. But it must never forget to consider these aspects in the perspective of religion: that is, in the name of the Gospel and for the Gospel, the Church has to be able to cross all frontiers of all kinds. That means as far as we are concerned that the Church must refuse to be enclosed by frontiers, and that it must make every effort to get outside its own dogmatic enclosures.

Yesterday and today 'translating the Gospel into a language and culture different from the original language and culture'[4] is an undertaking which is not without risks.

On the liturgical level, the situation has proved urgent. For fifty years our baptized members have prayed in Latin beside their Muslim brothers who prayed and continue to pray to God in Arabic, for the Quran cannot be translated. In proclaiming the translation of liturgical texts the Council has provoked a dual reaction: the fear that a variety of languages will bring about an uncontrollable diversity of interpretations; and the confusion of some Christians when faced with a celebration in the language of everyday life.

However, the fundamental intention of the liturgical renewal is clear: 'If God speaks to me, I should like him to speak in my own language'. Speeding up these translations which put the scriptural documents into various languages is to give priority to the living language over the written text, and to the consciousness of experience over formulations; it also means recognizing the great richness of revelation which our human words, above all those of a single culture, cannot exhaust. Finally, it means admitting that each of the human languages which arise from different cultural situations is capable of the Gospel, and capable of grace. Such a discovery applies both to the consciousness of the young communities and to the old churches.

If these situations can win the grace of the Gospel and once obtained, respond to it they pose by that very fact the problem of intra-ecclesial dialogue.

I do not mean, of course, dialogue between new and old churches. That is only one aspect of dialogue as far as we are concerned. The Church's essential structure is dialogue, and is so to the extent that the Word of God is living in the Church and ruling it. Then, just as grace is given to all mankind, so the Church becomes dialogue with human culture as a whole.

A NEW THEOLOGICAL UNDERSTANDING OF THE CHURCH

But is the meeting between our Church and our African cultures really taking place and will it continue to take place? In a general sense, there is cause to doubt that it has done so and will do so. There is the fact that the Church, not in declarations of principle but in factual instances, shows a reluctance to enter into our own cultural situations.

Anyone within the Christian communion might well ask if that is evidence of a deprecatory attitude due to dogmatic principles, or of a lack of tact and intelligence.[5] On the one hand, the Church at its centre seems in principle to be making great advances while showing great parsimony in their application; on the other hand, the young churches are both angry and enthusiastic. A typical example which I have already cited is the decree *Ad Gentes*. If you read that you will find the essential problems of African theology.

But is the experience of the young churches worth a theological translation? What I have said about pastoral perspectives is largely applicable to theology. Once theology is defined in traditional terms, we are in the area of theological experience, and that should be the place where the theologian, who is always a member of the community of faith, grounds his thought. The systems which have been so carefully developed hardly help one to gain access to this experience.

Where systematization is a rule, the vision of a theology of Christianity is imperative. Terms which were bearers of life have been fossilized. Hence we cannot be sure that the extraordinary experience of the young churches have had any effect on contemporary theology. The way in which it is received and expressed hardly seems to put in question certain definitions of the Church and of theology. By straightforward confiscation, the ruling Christian theology removes from the actual experience of the churches the benefit of their re-searches. Systematics begins to destroy the anthropological essence. That is the case in regard to the dualism of body and soul matter and spirit, person and community.

If we note the existence of several churches, with diverse experi-ences yet united in their longing for communion in faith, we must also recognize theological pluralism, which is itself the fruit of the fact that doctrinal truth cannot be stated, translated and expressed in the same way in all cultures. We have to leave to the Lord the freedom to revive other cultures, even if their response occurs in ways which seem of minor importance in comparison with the western model.

Perhaps, if we examine too minutely the faith experience of the young churches, we will harm their growth. What is admissible on the level of orthodoxy is difficult to take when it comes to theology. But the humility of our own theological knowledge should lead us to the actual realism of the Incarnation: there the Lord Jesus appears to upright hearts in search of light and truth, yet never imposes himself on them.

THEOLOGICAL EXPERIENCE AND DIALOGUE

Most of those who would like to practise theology in our young churches are, in methodology, training and often the presentation of their researches, the direct products of western theology. They have seldom had even a short introduction to the theological experience of the eastern churches. When they are asked to publicize their work abroad they often find themselves cut off from the living roots of their church communities. That is not surprising, since many of our works which have received academic praise are in fact second-hand products.

African theological experience has its own problems but does not have its own way of approaching its particular ground. Hence it tends to reach traditional and closed conclusions. The resulting impression can be that western theology has exhausted the theological possibilities and that all that has to be done is to exploit them. Closed dogmatic positions correspond to closed solutions, and these positions are main-tained by closed theologies which are more restrictive than Revelation itself.

We have to agree that 'No Christian theology can be simply the repetition of an existing theology, retouched for the needs of the moment'.[6]

In all good conscience, the specific experience of the young churches should find expression in legitimate theological movements and legiti-mate schools of theology. Is the blessing of other patented theologies necessary in such cases?

Of course to ignore those older theologies would be a theological

error, but to follow them slavishly, and to adopt their theological conclusions, would be just as wrong. We have to translate theologically the
actual experience of our young communities lest we keep them for ever
in a state of infantilism.

Yet even if a non-African is capable of talking theologically about an
actual situation in these young communities, it is doubtful whether in
his problematic, questions, and formulations, he can answer the expectations of those communities. In order to grasp what this implies, it is
enough to ask why Aristotle's intuitions proved more inspiring to St
Thomas than to St Bonaventure or to St Augustine.

Of course we must not deny the originality and authenticity of the
experience of the western churches; we would do so if we wished to
impose it on the African churches. Whatever the providential implications of the encounter between the Gospel and the Graeco-Latin world,
it cannot be the total and definitive expression of what the Gospel is
able to accomplish in another culture.

Without going so far as to defend a changing theology in a period of
transformation, we have to grasp and accept the progressive nature of
theological discourse.

The balanced systems of an unchanging theology do not of course
take into account the questioning of the Church's followers in the
world today. That dialogue seems to me indispensable.

NEW EXPERIENCE AND NEW FORMULAS

When questioning African theologians express their disagreement
with the positions of their colleagues elsewhere, annoyance results on
both sides and cultural sensitivity is held guilty. Of course Africans
pay attention to the positions of their counterparts in the fields of
economics, technology and politics. Why then are we faced with this
non-alignment of Africans in the Church?

Anyone can see in fact how inadequate any attempt is to draw a
parallel between situations in the Church and those in the political and
economic world. Of course, alignment for the same of major financial
aid can be restrictive but does not always mean that the consciousness
and conscience of the subservient party have been committed in depth
and irrevocably.

On the other hand, attitudes in the Church bring conscience and
ultimately basic choice into play. Can one subscribe to a thesis which is
logically satisfactory but which does not nourish life and conscience?
That is why, once ecclesial and fraternal communion with its demands
of truth and charity has been rendered secure, it is permissible to subject everything else to interrogation and analysis.

What is ultimately in question is reciprocal witness and not any rejection of the testimony of the old churches. It is a matter often of holding the same things, but not always in the same way, as Fr Congar has noted in regard to eastern theology. Just as other ecclesial communities exist on the basis of the same faith and yet with a different cultural population, the legitimacy of their life involves the legitimacy of their experience, and hence the legitimacy of their discourse.

But we must not confuse originality and universality. Is the experience of the western churches original and universal? I should be more inclined to acknowledge their originality, which translates the universality of the Church without however exhausting it.

A considerable effort is necessary here to redefine the Church while taking into account its new dimensions. This redefinition should respect the new awareness of the Church and its new image. It is the economy of salvation attempting to ground the faith dynamically in human cultures in all their diversity.

This kind of reflection is more appropriate if we wish to grasp the interdependence of western theology and cultures with their dominant Graeco-Latin and Roman-juridical emphases up to the transformation started by Vatican II.

The Church also has to become aware of its relation to specific local churches. The universal Church realizes that universality exists only through the medium of specific and local churches. It subsists in and through individual churches. The special constitution of the church of Rome does not make that any less true, as far as I can see.

That brings us to the realization that, with each generation and each particular socio-cultural phenomenon, theology has to reach a 'new understanding of the evangelical nature of the Church'.

The theologian has to appreciate that if he is not to traduce himself. This theological knowledge is understanding in and of the faith. In contact with the Word it reveals the countenance of God through various human situations, and grows by enabling the knowledge which a community has of its Lord to mature.

The theologian who seems to want to freeze theological conclusions tends to forget that the Word is still being sown. That is also true of the Church for which, in its advance towards the Lord, a thousand years are as a day. That is why, instinctively, many Africans are turning more to the Bible than to the Church's dogma; they hear the Word of God as the Gospel for them today. Full of respect for the western course of tradition, they know that other ways are possible inasmuch as mankind is converted by the Word of God.

It is perhaps in this sense that the young churches are evangelizing, or will evangelize, the old churches: not by lending them personnel and still less equipment, but by humble witness to a new understanding of the Church.

BIRTH OF A CHURCH AND OF A THEOLOGY

Faced with the actual problems of its ecclesial existence, theology rediscovers its birth and its growth in the Church. A theology is not created without imperfect approaches to its final state. Though it is aware of its theoretical conditions, the advance of African theology has not as yet defined the ways in which it will actually be realized.

Of course those centres of thought to which the young churches have particular access represent a major step on that road. They must articulate research into the experience of the actual communities which have been endowed by the Spirit, find an adequate formulation for it, and transmit the secular tradition of the *Ecclesia* in more apposite forms. These centres will prove their loyalty to Africa and favour communitarian thought and discourse.

The movement of the future will have a dialogal structure; it will constantly interact with the life of the Church and confront its contemporary experience.

The foregoing approach is essential. It consists in discovering Jesus Christ through re-reading the lines of our present socio-cultural situation in the light of the Gospel.

Methodology also requires renewal. Following the inspiration of the Fathers of the Church, we shall rethink our past and our present in terms of the history of the Church.

As far as the content is concerned, it must be more than the reformulation of existing theses as if they were exercises in a vacuum, from which nothing could develop, for theology arises from the discernment of spirits and from dialogue between preachers and evangelized Christians declaring their acceptance of and their faithful response to the Word of God. The life problems which awaken the questions and responses of the faithful ought by right to be treated first and not relegated to some subsidiary position. It is sad that in so many works, valuable and novel questions arise only outside their authors' closed dogmatic discourse.

Finally, the actual experience of the communities and their actual questions about the rôle of the Spirit and spirits in the world, communication between the visible and invisible worlds, and the material and eschatological dimensions of man and life, will be the major topics of this process of research and discovery.

Will our conversion to the Gospel be a factor in the renewal of our cultures and the millenarian Church? The affirmative reply I have summarized here is an act of hope from my heart as a believer and as pastor of a diocesan community. The evangelical revival taking shape in our African cultures and giving rise to these original Christian communities could be a source of rebirth for the millenarian Church rediscovering its other dimension as *Ecclesia*.

The Church, if it is to take part in a purification of cultures, must itself willingly undergo a process of purification in order to be truly in a position to hear the Word and the Spirit in the cultures and communities to which it gives birth. It can give fully only if it is ready to receive in depth, in the sense of undergoing real *kenosis* and fraternal openness on a really large scale.

There is much more that could be said; I have not, for instance, broached any of the areas of possible application of what I have put forward here; but everything that I have said has been declared in a spirit of total communion with the *Ecclesia* and in reference to it, in order to examine the future of these local communities and individual churches through which the Church is realized as the Ecclesia always called to self-renewal by the inspiration of the Creator Spirit.

Translated by V. Green

Notes

1. J. Mendelshon, *God-Allah and Juju in Africa*.
2. *Dei Verbum*, no. 2: 'Haec revelationis oeconomia fit gestis verbisque intrinsece inter se connexis'.
3. J. Gritti, *L'expression de la foi dans les cultures humaines* (Paris, 1975), pp. 67 ff.
4. D. von Allmen, *L'Evangile de Jésus-Christ* (Paris, 1972), pp. 324 ff.
5. Cf. my thesis, *Tierce Eglise, ma mère* (Paris, 1972).
6. D. von Allmen, *op. cit.*, p. 331.

René Laurentin

A Statistical Survey of Christians in Africa

AT the fourth Synod of Bishops in Rome, Mgr Sangu of Tanzania gave this statistical summary of the expansion of the Church in Africa:

> Christians number 149 million, forming 40% of the population of the continent (Muslims 41%; old tribal religions 17%).
> Catholics: 60 million, spread over 356 dioceses, make up 10% of the world's Catholics; the 17,180 priests, however, constitute only 4% of the total Catholic clergy.
> Christianity is growing: there are seven million more faithful every year, a growth rate double that of the population growth as a whole (p. 7).

The report ended with this prognosis:

> This expansion can continue, since there are still 35% of all Africans yet to hear the Good News, of which a third still adhere to ancient tribal religions.
> Catholics, 37 million strong today, will probably reach 50 million in ten years, and 100 million by the year 2000.

This report made a vivid impression and was one of the factors in the leadership shown by black African bishops at the 1974 Synod. But it immediately raises two questions:

1. What is the Catholic total: 37 million (p. 16) or 60 million (p. 7)?
2. How can Mgr Sangu speak of a growth rate of seven million per

annum when the *Vatican Statistical Annual* only gives one of between one and a half and two million? The reply to both questions (not made clear at the Synod) is the same: Mgr Sangu's report oscillated between two different statistical criteria, the Vatican one, which counts numbers of *baptized* Catholics,[1] and government sources, collated by Prof David Barrett of Nairobi, which counts all those who *declare themselves* Catholics, whether baptized or not.[2]

If one takes the second criterion, the *Christian* growth rate is indeed something like seven million annually, of which Catholics account for between three and four million.[3] If one takes the first, though, it is about two million.

The relationship between the different confessions is the following:

Catholics	59,600,000	16.2%
Protestants	45,200,000	12.3%
Orthodox	16,500,000	4.5%
Independent African Churches	15,000,000	4.12%
Anglicans	13,000,000	3.5%
Christian total	149,300,000	40.62%

There are two factors in the growth rate: population increase of 2.8% per annum, and conversions of 2.2%, giving a total of 5%. Progress over the last few years is best measured by the numbers of *baptized Catholics* in the whole Continent, for which the statistics are the most homogeneous and accurate:

*Parameters of Catholic Growth
in Africa*

Date	Population	Catholics	%
1969	346,006,000	38,046,000	11.0%
1970	343,910,000	39,728,000	11.6%
1971	359,709,000	41,746,000	11.6%
1972	368,932,000	42,943,000	11.6%
1973	378,935,000	44,135,000	11.6%
1974	391,078,000	46,292,000	11.8%

The effective number of those engaged in the apostolate has not kept pace with this growth, except for nuns; the number of priests and male religious is falling slightly, while the number of deacons remains insignificant.

Priests and Religious in Africa

Date	Priests	Deacons	Male Religious (non-ordained)	Nuns
1969	16,541	13	5,612	32,338
1970	17,142	16	5,780	33,360
1971	17,061	20	5,760	34,585
1972	17,043	31	5,601	35,142
1973	16,926	31	5,622	34,584
1974	16,428	35	5,441	34,157

The distortion reflects the fall in missionary aid resulting from the crisis in the countries supplying priests, religious and nuns. But the number of secular (non-religious) priests has continued to grow: by 54 in 1972, 160 in 1973, 4 in 1974. This growth is essentially due to the development of a native clergy, principally in the following countries:

Growth of Secular Clergy

Country	1972	1973	1974	Ordinations
1. Nigeria	+25	+50	+55	85
2. Tanzania	+21	+14	+36	26
3. Kenya	+7	+1	+11	10
4. Ghana	—	+10	+10	7
5. Zambia	+9	+3	+5	4
6. Upper Volta	+11	−3	+3	—

For sacraments and practice, the figures show a certain wavering, which indicates that sacramentalization (including baptism) has not kept pace with declared adherence to Christianity:

Baptisms, Ordinations and Marriages [4]

Date	Baptisms		Total	Ordinations	Marriages
	Child	Adult			
1969	1,409,432	714,120	2,123,552	176	185,017
1970	1,271,979	664,878	1,936,857	197	185,062
1971	1,333,851	708,885	2,042,736	201	182,553
1972	1,273,164	673,299	1,946,463	229	184,931
1973	1,238,106	648,801	1,886,907	210	185,663
1974	1,284,944	620,479	1,905,423	248	185,286

DIVERSITY IN AFRICA

Overall growth figures are not very significant unless seen in the context of the diversity of a continent which the mnemonics of geography have likened to a zebra's head. It is an apt symbol, for there is nothing less homogeneous than 'Africa'. Basically, it can be divided into three main areas: North, South and Central, with the islands a further consideration (and a number of sub-divisions into further zebra stripes always possible):

The Muslim North

(a) The Arab Countries

Country	Population Baptized 000's		%	Priests	Major Seminary Students	Ordinations
Algeria	16,275	66	0.4	300	1	0
Morocco	16,880	84	0.5	135	0	0
Tunisia	5,641	18	0.3	66	0	0
Egypt	36,416	137	0.4	394	90	2
Libya	2,346	17	0.7	6	0	0
Somalia	3,090	3	0.1	8	0	0
	80,648	325	0.4	909	91	2

The figures are taken from the latest available statistics: those for 1974.

(b) Black African Countries of the Sahara Region

Mauretania	1,290	6	0.5	9	0	0
Mali	5,561	46	0.8	324	15	2
Niger	4,476	12	0.3	23	1	0
	11,327	64	0.5	356	16	2

Total for these Muslim countries:

91,976	389	0.4	1,265	107	4

The Sudan (ex-British) is nine-tenths Muslim. It belongs mainly with the Muslim North, but its three Southern regions are populated by Christian Bantus:

Sudan	17,234	558	3.2	224	18	0

The South

Countries long under white domination, with growing black nationalism, and in a transitional period.

(a) Countries Still under White Domination

S. Africa	24,920	1,746	7.0	1,179	129	2
Rhodesia	6,100	594	9.7	120	80	2
	31,020	2,340	7.5	1,299	209	4

(b) Black Nations

Botswana	660	24	3.6	25	1	0
Lesotho	1,016	448	44.1	143	38	1
Namibia	692	128	18.5	71	7	0
Swaziland	478	42	8.8	35	3	0
Zambia	4,751	961	20.2	419	50	4
	7,597	1,603	21.0	693	99	5

(c) Former Portuguese Colonies, Independent Since 1974, Undergoing a Process of Radical Change

Angola	6,209	2,727	43.9	515	156	0
Mozambique	9,029	1,620	17.9	513	167	2

Cap Verde and Guinea-Bissau are in a similar situation.

The Centre

(a) French-Speaking Countries of the Western and Central Areas (of which Benin is Ex-Dahomey, while The Gambia Forms a Single Bishops' Conference with Senegal)

Benin	3,029	443	14.6	188	18	1
Ivory Coast	5,897	383	6.5	377	61	5
The Gambia	510	11	2.2	20	?	7
Upper Volta	5,897	383	6.5	372	96	4
Senegal	4,315	190	4.4	207	25	3
Togo	2,171	442	20.4	169	26	2
	21,819	1,852	8.5	1,333	226	22

Moving further to the centre, the first three countries of the next group share a common Bishops' Conference, A.C.E.C.C.T.

Congo Brazzaville	1,313	492	37.5	253	37	4
Cent. African Republic	2,076	291	14.0	191	26	1
Chad	3,949	214	5.4	119	9	0
Cameroon	6,282	1,569	25.0	723	154	2
Gabon	520	344	66.2	482	14	0
Zaire	24,222	10,346	42.7	2,408	514	18
Burundi	3,878	1,950	50.3	400	154	3
Ruanda	4,123	1,688	40.9	378	111	14
	46,363	16,894	36.4	4,954	1,019	42

(b) English-Speaking Black Nations Western Area

Ghana	9,607	1,172	12.2	355	14	7
Nigeria	61,270	3,737	6.1	892	881	85
Liberia	1,669	25	1.5	51	18	1
	72,546	4,934	6.8	1,298	913	93

Eastern Area: Five Countries Grouped in A.M.E.C.E.A.

Kenya	12,912	2,181	16.9	762	192	10
Malawi	4,900	972	19.8	324	80	5
Tanzania	14,763	2,878	19.5	1,284	506	26
Uganda	11,172	3,176	28.4	788	442	14
Zambia	4,751	961	20.2	419	50	4
(already included under The South)						
	48,498	10,168	20.9	3,577	1,270	59

This group has experienced considerable expansion between 1949 and 1974: 290% growth in baptisms; 314% in priests, and a still higher increase in the number of bishops.

Other Countries

(a) The Islands

Madagascar	7,500	1,764	23.5	689	93	11
Mauritius	872	268	30.7	90	7	0
Reunion	490	450	91.8	120	9	2
Seychelles	3,707	54	1.5	27	0	0

(b) Others

Ethiopia	27,239	186	0.7	482	117	3
Liberia	1,669	25	1.5	51	18	1
(already included)						
Sao Tome	79	66	83.5	13	0	0
Equatorial Guinea	305	280	91.8	44	39	1

CONCLUSION

Africa is at the crossroads. The most striking statistical facts are these:

1. The population of Africa is growing steadily: by about ten million per annum.

2. The number of baptized Catholics is keeping pace with this growth: increasing by about two million each year, 11% of the population in 1969, increasing to 11.8% in 1974.

3. The number of those who call themselves Catholics without being baptized is far higher still. In Kenya, for example, where overall Christian growth has been about 500,000 p.a. in the years surveyed, David Barrett's statistics give, for 1972:

1,900,000 baptized Catholics

1,500,000 unbaptized Catholics (*op. cit.,* n. 3, pp. 173–5).

Barrett's conclusion is that the Churches are not succeeding in making sacramental initiation keep up with the numbers of those who feel attracted to Christ and Christianity. This does not apply only to the Catholic Church, but to all Christian bodies, division among which is no doubt at least partly responsible for the weak institutional adherence.

4. African Catholics, numbering 23 million in 1960, will number 175 million in the year 2000, according to Walter Bühlmann, *The Miro Church* (London & New York, 1975), p. 37, who borrows the following table (without explicit acknowledgement) from Barrett, in *International Review of Mission* (January, 1970), p. 47:

No. of (000,000's)	1900	1930	1950	1970	2000
Catholics	1	6	14	45	175
Protestants	1	4	9	29	110
Orthodox, Coptic	2	5	8	14	32
Independent African Churches	0	1	3	9	34
Total	4	16	34	97	351

Africa is an example of the growing importance of the Church of the Third World, which will soon become the majority:

In 1900: 15% of the Church
In 1965: 37%
In 2000: 58%.

This projection is linked to the fact that the population of Africa grew by 89.05% from 1930 to 1960: a slower growth rate than that of Latin America, the Catholic continent, with 125%, but higher than that of Asia (62.94%), or Europe (25%). As Bühlmann concludes: 'The migration of the Church towards the Southern hemisphere is then an indisputable fact, an historic ecclesial event at the same time as an undreamt-of possibility'.

EVOLUTIONARY FACTORS

In view of the importance of this phenomenon, we should evaluate the external and internal factors that condition future development.

(a) *External Obstacles*. There are two factors external to the Church that hinder its development:

1. Ethnic rivalries: but the peace-promoting and integrating role of Christianity in these conflicts redounds to its prestige. In the current situation of extreme difficulty and tragic conflicts in Africa, this is something that has surely yet to bear its full fruit.

2. Limitation of religious freedom affects the Church under three types of régime:

(i)   White-dominated countries. There is the case of Mgr Lamont, sentenced to ten years hard labour in Rhodesia.

(ii) Marxist, or rather Marxist-type African regimes: Guinea, where Mgr Tchidimbo is still in prison; Benin and the former Portuguese colonies.

(iii) Authoritarian régimes that see the Catholic Church as a foreign institution, a western intruder, an obstacle to Africanization. The difficulties posed by these, in Zaïre and Amin's Uganda, have decreased over the past few years.

These obstacles have on the whole provided a trial from which the Church has emerged strengthened. But African Christians have the right to support from all the churches. One must hope that the support of the Holy See, which undoubtedly has a part to play, is not used as an alibi for basic Christian solidarity, in all its dimensions, popular and ecumenical.

(b) Internal Difficulties.   The internal problems of the Church are more serious:

1. The imbalance between the growth in the people and the overall fall in numbers of clergy, since the slight increase in native clergy in some countries is far from compensating for the decline in missionary help.

Celibacy should not be seen as *the* cause of this situation, since it also applies in confessions with married pastors. It is one factor among others, of which the most decisive are faith and apostolic zeal. But it does have particular relevance to Africa, where celibacy strikes no cultural echoes, as it does in Asia, for example.

Furthermore, Africa, with a mere 35 deacons, has shown no interest in the diaconate, unlike South America, with 299, Central America, with 28, or North America, where the number has gone from 1,000 in the same year of 1974 to over 2,000 today.

2. The African churches are still in many ways foreign churches: their institutions, leaders and personnel are still European. This problem is not new, and exists wherever a central authority seeks to impose uniformity. This is why we have never succeeded, in Latin America in the first place and now in Africa, in forming an even remotely sufficient native clergy. With one or two exceptions such as Mexico and Colombia, the number of priests is infinitesimal (less than one per 5,000 faithful) and the proportion of foreign priests is often over 50%.

Africa is no exception, with a majority of foreign priests.[5]

At the level of bishops, Africanization has passed the fifty per cent mark: considerably more in Black Africa. There has also been considerable progress in native female religious vocations, as the following table (from *Annuaire de l'Eglise en Afrique francophone 1974–75)* shows:

African Women Religious: Statistics for Four Countries

Country	1900	1920	1940	1960	1972
Senegal	28	24	31	87	92
Upper Volta	—	—	37	128	292
Ruanda	—	1	97	222	200
Madagascar	—	—	136	358	788

At the catechist level, the Church is 100% native, and this is the very basis of the African Church, the mainspring of its stabilization and expansion. The catechists and other lay people in charge of small communities are the guarantors of Christianity in the people. Many African priests and bishops are sons of catechists, and the admirable quality of many of them, their faith and prayerfulness, made a deep impression in Rome in the Holy Year.

How many of them are there? It is impossible to find out, as the definitions are so various: full-time and part-time, qualified or not, regularly paid or supported in some other way, either with money or goods. In some countries, the traditional local communities have granted them a parcel of land, so that they can at least support themselves.

The number would seem to be in the region of 100,000 (given that there are reckoned to be about 150,000 in Asia and Africa, of which seven out of ten are in Africa.[6] Fr René Cordie, director of *Aide aux Missions d'Afrique*, puts the number at 70,000, but without specifying how he arrives at this figure (*La Croix*, 23 November 1976, p. 7).

Africanization of the Church, prophetically launched by Piux XI, and encouraged by Paul VI on his visit to Kampala, is now a living reality, but an elusive and complex one. It implies a *quality* that statistics cannot define. Statistics have their limits.

Translated by Paul Burns

Notes

1. *Annuarium statisticum Ecclesiae:* six volumes published, 1969–74, with statistics up to 31 December of the year of the title. This statistical office, set up after the Council at the Secretariat of State, is continually improving the standards and presentation of its publications, which can now be taken as definitive. From 1973, the text is in Latin, English and French. These volumes are the source of the figures given in this article, except where indicated otherwise.

2. 'I have obtained the religious censuses of governments, in which the term "Catholic" refers to a broader group: all those who *call themselves* Catholic. This latter category is considerably greater than the number of baptized Catholics': letter from Dr David Barrett to the author, 10 June 1976.

Dr Barrett has published *Frontier Situations for Evangelization in Africa, 1972: A Survey Report*, and is currently preparing a *World Christian Handbook*, a statistical survey of Christianity, which will give figures for all the major Churches according to different criteria, e.g., placing those for baptized Christians alongside those who just declare themselves Christians—a widespread phenomenon today, not only in Africa, but also, for example, in Japan.

3. D. Barrett, 'The Expansion of Christianity in Kenya, AD 1900–2000', in *Kenya Churches Handbook, 1973*. 'Five hundred thousand inhabitants of this country embrace the Christian faith each year', he claims there.

4. There is an interesting cultural comparison to be made on the basis of the figures for 1974: the total number of baptized Catholics in Africa—46,292,000—was slightly below that for the USA—46,608,000—but the number of baptisms each year in the U.S.A. was half that of Africa—942,103 against 1,900,423. On the other hand, the USA had twice the African number of Catholic marriages—389,982 against 185,286—which proves that the canonical

institution of marriage is badly adapted to native African customs. For ordina-
tions, the USA had three times the African number—767 against 248.

5. In Zambia, for example, a relatively prosperous country, there are 440
priests, of whom only 59 are Zambians, and the others 'expatriates', i.e.,
non-African. There are 171 brothers, of whom only 9 are Zambian; 594 sisters,
of whom 127 are Zambian and 467 from outside. It is only at the level of
catechists, 811, all Zambian, that the Church can be said to be native. Four out
of nine bishops are also Zambian. See F. J. Verstralen, *An African Church from
Missionary Dependence to Mutuality in Mission: A Case Study on the Roman
Catholic Church in Zambia* (Leiden, 1975), vol. I, pp. 56–57.

6. The Congregation for the Evangelization of Peoples has published numerous studies of catechists, notably, *Catéchistes en Afrique, en Asie et en Océanie*
(Rome, Commission for Catechesis and Catechists, 62 pp.), which gives wise
directives for this important sector. But the studies do not risk statistics. The
publishers of the *Annuarium* are planning an enquiry with the aim of integrating
available figures, but there are formidable difficulties to be overcome. The
figures in this article are taken from many partial studies undertaken by the
Pontifical Congregation for the Missions.

Harold Turner

Independent Churches of African Origin and Form

THE modern African Christian community stretches well beyond the Christians connected with missions or belonging to the national churches these have founded. Estimates vary, but there are probably between five and ten million people in Black Africa (i.e., south of the Sahara) who regard themselves as Christians and who find their spiritual home in what have come to be called the African independent churches. These have been founded by Africans who usually have some kind of Christian background and who have developed forms of Christianity expressed in African cultural ways to meet the needs of African peoples as they themselves determine. In general, the longer the Christian presence in an area the larger the number of independent churches. Thus there are perhaps some 3000 in South Africa, in Ghana about 500, some 300 or so in Nigeria, numbers of the same order in Zaïre, and many in Western Kenya, the Ivory Coast, and so on. Each of these amounts to a separate denomination with its own structures and membership, and while some consist of a single small congregation others embrace scores of thousands of members and may have spread into a number of tribes and into several different nations. The largest is the great Kimbanguist Church (Eglise du Jésus Christ par le prophète Simon Kimbangu); it may have well over a million members, has spread into some six countries in central Africa, and in 1969 was admitted as a member of the World Council of Churches. Certain cautions, however, apply to the recognition of all these bodies as 'churches' in any Christian or theological sense. The majority may perhaps be so accepted on the basis of their intention rather than their achievement, for they understand themselves as African forms of Christianity founded by the prophets and leaders who have been given by the God of the Scriptures to his African people. At the same time there is remarkably little hostility to missions and the older churches, for it is recognized that these first brought the Christian faith to Africa; on the other hand they are regarded as too dependent on Western forms, Western critiques, and Western assistance.[1]

THE RANGE OF NEW RELIGIOUS MOVEMENTS

The independent churches should be seen as representing the Christian end of a spectrum of forms that embrace other types of new religious movements that have also arisen in response to the encounter with the Christian religion and Western societies. Thus there are 'Hebraist' movements which correspond to the religion of biblical Israel (such as the Bayudaya, i.e., 'the Jews', in Uganda, the Israelites in South Africa, and the God's Kingdom Society in Nigeria). Then there are syncretist movements that deliberately attempt a fusion of traditional African and Christian elements; such are the Bwiti cult in Gabon, the Déima cult in Ivory Coast, and the former 'Church' of the Sacred Heart in Zambia. Beyond these, at the other end of the spectrum, there are what may be called 'neo-primal' cults which are attempting to renew traditional African religions by certain Christian borrowings; we may name the Aruosa cult and Godian religion in Nigeria, and the cult of Mumbo and the Dini ya Misambwa (religion of the Ancestors) in Kenya. These other forms must be kept in mind for several reasons: at certain points they reveal a quite specific break from traditional ways (e.g., in the rejection of magic, and the acceptance of a single personal god); they may represent the true nature of bodies wrongly regarded as independent churches; and they themselves may change in the course of time and so move along the spectrum to the independent church form, which is certainly the most numerous in Africa today. Only a very few movements are 'messianic' in the sense of following a 'Black Messiah', an African founder who has become a rival or replacement of Jesus Christ, for the term "Black Moses" or "Black Elijah" is a more accurate description of the usual attitudes to the founders.[2]

CAUSAL FACTORS

Most of these bodies have arisen within the last hundred years, and with increasing frequency in the course of this century. Their causes[3] are legion, for economic, political, social and cultural factors have all been at play, and the particular forms of these in the colonial situation have been especially significant. In the earlier part of the century, before trade unions and political parties were in existence, the desire for political independence and economic betterment joined with the search for an independent and African Christianity as part of the dynamic of these movements. Now they tend to be a-political and their religious motivation is clearer. Basically this may be described as a deep yearning for spiritual independence from the West and for responsibility before God in his direct dealings of blessing and power with his African peoples; in consequence a great African Church will grow, will be recognized as truly Christian by the rest of the world, and will make its own special contribution to the Churches in other continents. To this deep and often sub-conscious motive many other more conscious and specific motives are joined. These include disappointment with Western Christianity as lacking the full power of its own Gospel to deal with the needs of African peoples for deliverance from evil forces, for healing and divine guidance, and for intimate fellowship with one another and, in many areas, with the ancestors also. The prominence of spiritual healing, by prayer, faith, fasting and holy water and without use of Western medicines, reveals a sense of the inadequacy of the older churches and the Western medicines associated with them to deal with psychic disorders and the spiritual causes of sickness. There is also a common disappointment with the Bible brought by the missions insofar as it has not revealed the supposedly spiritual secrets of the power and wealth of the whites; hence the new revelations given to founding prophets when they 'die' and visit heaven and return with a new teaching or ritual, or even with a new 'book'. Then again, Western denominations that arose only in modern times with Wesley, Calvin or Luther, or Henry VIII (!), or even with the eleventh century split between the East and Rome, these are regarded as only man-made churches, and the search continues for the true original church of the New Testament or even of Moses or Adam. These endeavours, however misguided or historically perverse, are attempts to bring the biblical world view into practical relationship with contemporary African needs.

THE ATTITUDES OF THE OLDER CHURCHES

Our reactions to these independent churches should be governed by recognition of the fact that none of these would have occurred if the Christian faith had not come to Africa. To this extent they are the creation and therefore the offspring and the responsibility of the older Christian community, which is faced with a new mission and ecumenical 'front' across Black Africa.[4] It is a mission front insofar as the apprehension of the Gospel in these bodies is confused, distorted or heretical, and especially in relation to those movements classified as Hebraist, syncretist, or neo-primal. This mission task is a novel and delicate one for it relates to bodies that have already made their own response, according to their own understanding, to the Christian encounter, and that may regard themselves as a new form of Christianity for Africans. It is also an ecumenical front insofar as it is possible to accept many of these bodies as churches and admit them to Christian councils or fellowship. At this point there has been a dramatic change of attitude since the early 1960s when the independent churches were still misunderstood, rejected, or even bitterly attacked as pagan syncretistic defections. In spite of this the independent churches have continued to reach out for recognition and fellowship, and especially for help with the training of their own ministries. Now they are to be found in many Christian councils, and a number of pioneering projects have started to bring help with biblical study and theological training. The Mennonite Church of the USA has the most extensive experience here, having worked in this way with these churches in Nigeria, Ghana, Botswana, Swaziland, etc.; Canadian Baptists are working in another way in Kenya. The Christian Institute of Southern Africa helped in the establishment of a training school for the ministers of an association of independents, and with correspondence courses; a group of white teachers from various churches helps to staff the theological college of the Kimbanguists; an Afrikaaner missionary in Rhodesia has been the catalyst for the establishment of a Conference of independents, and for theological education by extension; and a number of seminaries have admitted students from the independent churches to train alongside their own ordinands—notably the Lutheran seminary in Natal.

THEOLOGICAL IMPORTANCE[5]

There is considerable theological significance in the existence and in the nature of these independent churches. In the first place there is no similar reaction to African peoples to their encounter with Islam. This says something important about both the nature of Islam and the nature of Christianity, for the latter has produced a similar range of new religious movements among the tribal peoples of other major culture areas outside Africa. Here we can do no more than suggest that there is a deep affinity between the tribal worlds and the world of the Bible and the Christian faith. Then, further, there are numerous and even new heresies in these independent churches. In many the Christology is weak and the sacrament of Holy Communion is absent; in others baptism has become a denominational admission rite or a purification or healing ritual that can be repeated as necessary. A few reject one or other of the two biblical Testaments. Many accept dreams, trances, and visions as new revelations without any Christian critique. Prayer and use of holy water become new magic rituals, and healing and practical blessings are expected as of right now, or through the power of the Holy Spirit operating out of all reference to the Trinity. There is an evasion of the Cross and a foreshortening of the Christian hope so that the consummation is to be enjoyed in the present; one utopian movement even claimed to have conquered death and refused to admit that any member had ever died. Much of this, of course, is only too familiar in Christian history, but there is often a special African cultural twist to these heresies, and herein lies their special contribution to the development of the much-talked-of African theology. The latter will emerge from the struggle of the whole Christian community in Africa with its own problems, and especially with its own heresies as found more clearly in the uninhibited independent churches. In the third place these independents reveal the culture-bound nature of Western doctrinal formulations and theology, and especially in the doctrine of the Church. In deciding whether or not these bodies are to be called 'churches' and so admitted to councils of Christian churches we find that the traditional 'notes', 'marks', or signs of the Church to be found in the creeds, confessions and declarations of Western Christianity are of little help. Other more dynamic and less institutionalized criteria have to be found, criteria that will take account of the nature of the Church as it is emphasized among the independents. These present themselves as a 'place to feel at home', a personalized community of love within African societies, an accepting community ready to include polygamists and to find a place for ancestors, and to maintain the authentic values of social life in traditional African cultures. And finally, we must be prepared to take seriously those independent churches which regard themselves as a new African reformation of the faith as over against the Western Christianity of the missions and the national churches. These are seen as having lost the full power of the Gospel, or of the Holy Spirit, and as being formal structures where the sense of community is weak, where real individual pastoral care is rare, where the laity and especially women have little place, and where the apostolic commission to carry the faith to other tribes and nations in Africa or beyond is ignored. All these represent weak spots in the older churches of Africa, and at many of these points the record of the better independent churches presents a striking contrast.

CONTRIBUTIONS TO DEVELOPMENT[6]

In addition to their theological significance these movements possess considerable sociological importance and are making a contribution towards the modernization of Africa. Although we have spoken of them as 'churches' in the theological sense, their diverse social forms cannot all be embraced within this term when used in this different context. There is the common earlier more inchoate form of a prophet movement which may pass over into the church form in the sense of a denomination with congregations; alternatively it may issue in a new total or comprehensive community, a new holy village, 'Jerusalem', 'Paradise', or 'Zion City' with its own economic base; or again the result may be ancillary cults whose members come for benefits unavailable in the older churches to which they still belong; or where there may be no more than clientele focussed on a powerful healer or prophet and with no corporate cultic activities. This variety is one contribution towards the establishment of pluralism and voluntarism in African societies, and towards the distinction between religious and political organization and activity that is vital for the future of the continent. Equally vital is the introduction of the ascetic element in Christian form into African cultures where this has not been prominent. Over against the current conspicuous consumption that often marks the new élites, and capital-intensive industrialization that produces luxury consumer goods such as cigarettes and beer and so makes a negative contribution to the development of most African countries, the independent churches usually present a rigorous and puritan ethic that encourages simpler living and often bans alcohol and tobacco; their members therefore are liable to be preferred as employees. But even more important than these specific contributions to development there is the great mental and spiritual activity associated with the entry into a new faith, new community, and new way of life which demands a drastic repudiation of magic and the spirit cults and offers a great new hope for the future. All this brings the deep personal and cultural changes and the new incentives and dynamics without which there can be no entry into the more developed modern world. Here secular and spiritual development are combined and the independent churches are making their own contribution at the grassroots level to the future of Africa.

Notes

1. For the only major survey, see D. B. Barrett, *Schism and Renewal in Africa* (Nairobi, 1968).

2. On messianism, see B. G. M. Sundkler, *Bantu Prophets in South Africa* (London, 2nd ed. 1961), pp. 323–37. This is the pioneering study of independent

churches; see also his *Zulu Zion and Some Swazi Zionists* (Lund & London, 1976).

3. For causes, and also the world range of similar movements see H. W. Turner, 'Tribal Religious Movements', New *Encyclopaedia Britannica* (Chicago, 1974), vol. 18, pp. 697–705.

4. See development of this theme in H. W. Turner, 'A Further Dimension for Missions', *International Review of Mission* 62 (1973), pp. 321–37.

5. For further theological reflections see H. W. Turner, 'The Contribution of Studies on Religion in Africa to Western Religious Studies', in M. E. Glasswell & E. Fashole-Luke (eds.), *New Testament Christianity for Africa and the World* (London, 1974), pp. 169–78; also G. Oosterwal, *Modern Messianic Movements* (Elkhart, Indiana, 1973).

6. See also H. W. Turner, 'The Place of Independent Religious Movements in the Modernization of Africa', *Journal of Religion in Africa* 2 (1969), pp. 45–63; *idem*, 'African Independent Churches and Education', *Journal of Modern African Studies* 13 (1975), pp. 295–308; also research sponsored by a Catholic mission—M. F. Perrin Jassy, *La Communauté de Base dans les Eglises Africaines* (Bandundu, Zaïre, 1970), Eng. trans. *Basic Community in the African Churches* (New York, 1973).

Luc Moreau

The Chances of a Dialogue between Christianity and Islam in Black Africa

POST-CONCILIAR Catholic circles still see the dialogue between Christianity and Islam in terms that are far too abstract. When we talk about 'dialogue', we talk about persons, groups, and relations between communities, and here we are concerned with Moslems and Christians. But there can be no dialogue between doctrines and theologies. This is why the relations differ very much from one region to another: from the Middle East, where Islam has had the upper hand over the Christians right through history, to North Africa where Christians today are strangers left behind by a period of colonial occupation.

In black Africa very different situations still prevail, particularly in the West: there is no heavy backlog of historical conflict between the two religious beliefs. This makes it easier to see various ways into the future, but it still requires the will to open them up. The fact is that in a certain way confrontation and painful encounters at least make people know something about each other and may lead to some attempts at reconciliation, but where people ignore each other there is a danger that they will remain just indifferent to each other. And this is the situation which has prevailed in black Africa till today.

In what follows I shall steer clear of attempting a genuine analysis of opportunities for dialogue today or in the near future. I prefer first of all to bring out the original features which marked the relations between Christians and Muslims in the past, then go on to say something about what is attempted today, and finally try to outline what the future may bring.

NO HEAVY BACKLOG OF HISTORICAL CONFLICT

If Islam and Christianity both originated outside the world of the African Negro, the development of the respective communities has been for a long time widely apart, both in time and geographically. By the eleventh century Islam, penetrating from Upper Egypt and the Maghreb, had already made solid contact with black Africa. The Christians arrived only five centuries later on the western coasts: real Christian communities only appeared in the nineteenth century. Even so it has to be admitted that these communities were predominantly foreign and half-caste. In general, the missionaries built up their Christian communities where there was no Islamic presence, trying in this way to overtake the speed of Muslim expansion. Only where there were landing-stages and ports were relationships developed, sometimes close ones, as at Saint-Louis (Senegal) or on the island of Gorée, where there are mixed families that go a long way back.

It would be untrue to deny that there was any conflict: a competitive situation spawned local rivalries, sometimes quite sharp ones; there were quarrels between church-bells and minarets, but there never was any organized crusade.

It is even interesting to mention that there were moments of very positive relationships where either Christians or Moslems took the initiative.

There was, for instance, Mgr Truffet, Vicar Apostolic of the two Guineas in 1847, who, a fervent ultramontane, did not want to be linked with the colonial administration. When in difficulty, he preferred to approach the Muslim authorities of Dakar, rather than the French army. His letters, recently published,[1] show an open mind: 'We, apostles, have to bring the truth to these regions, not war'. While he recognizes the fact that the Muslims refuse to be converted to Christianity, he is keen on a friendly relationship. He mentions the sympathetic reception given him by the notables of Dakar, and highly praises Sulaiman, nephew of the great Serigne, who gave him lessons in Wolof. Obviously, this is not a matter of dialogue as we understand it today but it shows that those missionaries showed an esteem and respect which were not always present later on.

On the part of the Muslims, other recent studies lead us to an original work by a Senegalese scholar, El Hadjj Moussa Kamara (1863–1943), written towards 1940 and entitled: 'Agreement between the Christian religion and Islam is almost perfect'.[2] Already in his introduction the author explains that he has been led to write this little book 'because of his love of concord and his hate of discord'. And he concludes his work with, as the last line: 'My God, bring the Christian religion and ours together'. His reflections start with an encounter he had with nuns whom he asked questions about their prayer: he was most struck by the similarities with his own prayer. After recalling the good relations which existed between the first generations of Muslims with the Christians of those days, he looks for the hidden meaning of Christian expressions in order to give the reader to understand that we are perhaps much closer to each other than we think at present.

During the same period there died in Bandiagara, Upper Volta, Tierno Bokar Salif Tall, a Tijan scholar, of Hamallist persuasion, whose teaching was centred not only on the sense of God, but on the love which human beings owe each other. On these lines he advocated a broad ecumenism, particularly among the 'people of the Book', Muslims, Jews and Christians. According to one trend of classical Islamic theology the different religions are for him, too, but different ways which lead to the one worship of the one God. This peaceful preaching of 'the wise man of Bandiagara' is well known today thanks to his disciple Amadou Hampate Ba[3] who for many years has been labouring towards the development of the dialogue between Christians and Muslims, ever since he made contact with the White Fathers of Mali and particularly Theodore Monod.

THE WILL TO COME TOGETHER TODAY

Relations between Muslim and Christian communities became particularly cool in recent times during the period of decolonization, between 1950 and 1960.

On the Catholic side, the hierarchy gathered strength from the development of the local churches, but most of the officials were still Europeans. Among the missionaries two attitudes dominated the approach towards African Islam. On the one hand, this Islam could not be taken as truly representative of Islam as such because too much affected by African traditions, and, because of this, no time should be wasted and the matter should be taken seriously as soon as possible. On the other hand, as the young generations were trained in Egypt or in the Maghreb and were politically restless, there was reason to fear revolutionary movements, tainted by Marxism. This meant that in the Christian communities, still very young, attitudes developed of mistrust, fear, and even contempt.

On the Muslim side opposite feelings tended to harden, faced as they were by churches that grew in strength without shedding the power of western influence.

Yet, at the same time, particularly among the students, there was no lack of moves to meet and co-operate, and what with political independence on the one part and Vatican II on the other, irreparable conflicts were avoided.[4]

In order, therefore, to understand what is going on today, one has to take account at the same time of a long tradition of indifference and lack of understanding together with the more recent cooling-off, along with the existing attempts at more open attitudes and the new situation created by the liberation of peoples and churches.

What is happening today is that Africans, responsible for their own economic, political, social, cultural and religious future, are re-discovering each other. Unfortunately, life never allows us to start with a clean slate: there is always a past we have to get beyond.

And so it is that for some ten to fifteen years people are learning bit by bit to recognize each other, timidly or boldly, but most often in the ordinary run of every day life. And so they learn to live together without having to tell themselves: 'I am now doing something about the dialogue between Islam and Christianity''. In fact links are quietly being forged at grass-roots level.

After the Council, what was done privately or sometimes secretly, was often taken up more publicly, and officially. In every country the Church organized its own team of specialists to pool and examine the experiments and to see what the next steps might be. Since 1966 meetings have taken place at the level of French-speaking West Africa. What was immediately the easiest and most urgent task was to provide information and training to make Islam and the Muslims better understood: among Christians, according to their needs, meetings of militants, or regular courses in the seminaries and the centres for catechist training.[5]

But where Christians and Muslims live constantly in close contact with each other problems arise at once, such as the question of religious teaching, or mixed marriages and families. Here an attempt is made to approach these problems in a more positive manner than in the past.[6] The very sincerity of the determination to open up a better relationship has led to discussions with the Muslims themselves: in Niamey, Abidjan and elsewhere there are occasional or regular meetings of high quality, in the seriousness of the debate as well as in the friendliness of the relationship. We could also give many examples of things undertaken in common, whether it was a matter of fighting the drought in the Sahel, or of organizing cultural activities among young people, or producing a religious broadcast.

According to the country and the Church's situation in a given country, or the Muslim presence there, the relations which are beginning to be built up take on various forms, not always sufficiently thought out, nor sufficiently clear in purpose. But this is perhaps preferable to a too rapidly neatly constructed theory and the over-centralization of the various undertakings. There are vast differences between Senegal or Mali, where the indigenous churches live in an environment where the Muslims are in the majority, and Niger or Mauritania where the Christians are strangers: in Senegal they are among compatriots, in Niger they are guests.

In short, at present we have to recognize that in the last few years the climate has greatly changed; fresh undertakings have been born which have a future. But it is only a beginning, a breaking of the ice. Nevertheless, these fresh undertakings are scattered, dotted about, even though the dots are becoming more numerous. And the restraints are still there, and not merely due to the ill will of the people. In Christian communities which are still too young the freedom of an open approach often lacks pliability, even if only because of cautiousness among the pastors.

Where peoples are spread out over vast spaces complex influences inevitably come into play. If the religious factor does not directly influence the political life of the various states, there are strong pressures, without counting the foreign powers which are tempted to use Christians or Muslims in turn. The risk of future tensions is not illusory, as shown during some recent crises concerned with oil. But the reactions at the time have proved the maturity and coolness of the partners, and, in spite of some very unhelpful positions taken up by someone like Gadhafi in 1975, African bishops took part in the colloquium which was held at Tripoli one year later.[7]

FORGING LINKS FOR THE FUTURE

Insofar as the communities will be able to take their dialogue right into the great issues which beset the continent of Africa, the links will become stronger and more promising, even beyond the black world, and only achieving a renewal of the dialogue between Islam and Christianity which is still far too exclusively limited to Arabs and Europeans. The collaboration, so far achieved, will only have a future if believers are determined to witness at the heart of that world which is now in the making. Therefore they will have to consider such problems as the Muslim author Mamadou Dia has brought up in his significant work, *Islam, sociétés africaines et culture industrielle.*[8]

Both Muslims and Christians share the fears and the hopes of an urban and industrial society. Both have to examine the Negro-African authenticity of their faith. But they will do so in their different ways. This common research has to take place on several levels at the same time. I found this out myself when I took part in the 'workshops' which took place at Dakar in 1970 and of which Dr Doudou Gueye was the centre.

We became aware of a whole network of lines of thought and sensitivity which was shared by Christians trained in classical Catholic theology and Muslims trained in Arab universities. We all had similar reactions when it came to the problems of society created by technology and the modern sciences. This field has vast possibilities for fruitful exchanges, and we should not be afraid of progress. And yet, in the end the style of debating was no different from a debate in Algiers or Paris, and we would have been in danger of ignoring Africa if we had not had with us members of Muslim brotherhoods and Catholics concerned about 'African theology'.

Here, so it seems to me, we have a whole field of original and urgent problems which demand common research: the concern with African theology is common to both sides. In so far as this religious reexamination wants to see itself as starting from the roots, from the practice of believers, all believers, the inclusion of popular Islam and its religious confraternities, underrated for such a long time, could be extremely fruitful. It is obviously not a question of withdrawing into ancient folklore, but rather of studying the evolution of those religious movements right up to the present. As I said at the beginning, Islam has been a long-standing guest of Africa: the cross-fertilization proceeded very freely, without the traumas of a quick and authoritarian catechization, and without any insistence on Arabization. Without wishing to draw any lessons at this point, Christian cannot just ignore this long experience of his Muslim compatriots.

What is, fundamentally, the real issue? In my opinion it is that we must change our usual way of looking at religious beliefs as if they are societies which are set up once for all and as such must come closer together.

After having been separated by boundaries (and not only political ones) which have been imposed on them from outside, Africans want to recover themselves again among each other in order to understand and develop their future prospects. Among themselves, as Africans, they are led to find out how their religious faith can in truth be light and life for their peoples today and in the future.

The dialogue between Muslims and Christians is certainly based on the same one God, the God of Abraham, but it is also based on their common African roots and their common historic destiny. This is how the problem was already formulated in 1961 at a colloquium of the African Society of Culture in Abidjan.[9]

In this perspective religious dialogue among Africans can not only contribute a way of transforming the dialogue between Islam and

Christians, which has been monopolized by westerners and Arabs, but will also pave the way for far more open-ended encounters:[10] all Muslims are not Arabs and all Christians are not westerners: there are African Christians, Eastern Christians, etc. As Africans continue to meet each other among Muslims and Christians, it will be the Muslims and Christians beyond Africa who will also be forced to re-examine the rigidity of their own religious structures (both mental and canonical) in order to resume their dialogue afresh, a dialogue henceforth based on our common historical and quite simply human responsibilities.

Translated by T. Weston

Notes

1. Paule Brasseur, 'A la recherche d'un absolu missionnaire: Mgr. Truffet, vicaire apostolique des Deux-Guinées (1812–1847)' in *Cahiers d'Etudes africaines* 58, XV-2, pp. 259–85.

2. Amar Samb, Director of the Institut Fondamental d'Afrique noire (Dakar), published a translation of it in the Bulletin of that Institute: *B.I.F.A.N.* (B), 1973.

3. Amadou Hampate Ba and Marcel Cardaire, *Tierno Bokar, le Sage de Bandiagara* (Paris, 1957).

4. It is enough to recall the utterances of Mgr Marcel Lefebvre, archbishop of Dakar, and his regrettable article in *La France Catholique* of 18 December 1959, 'Du croissant à l'étoile'.

5. E.g., at the seminary of Sébikotane (Senegal) or at the Institut Supérieur de Culture Religieuse (Ivory Coast).

6. Cf. the 'Pastoral Document on mixed marriages' of the Episcopal Conference of Senegal-Mauritanie (April 1972).

7. This refers to the 'Séminaire du dialogue islamo-chrétien' which took place in the capital of Libya from 1–6 February, 1976.

8. Dakar, 1975.

9. 'Colloque sur les religions' (Abidjan, 5–12 April, 1961).

10. Cf. Mamadou Dia, *op. cit.*, pp. 63–64.

Contributors

JACOB MEDÉWALÉ AGOSSOU was born at Hondji, Dahomey. He is a Eudist priest. His doctoral thesis was on conceptions of man and God in South-Dahomeyian consciousness. He teaches religious anthropology and Christian origins at the Anyama Major Seminary and ethno-sociology at the Higher Institute of Religious Worshop and Practice.

F. EBOUSSI BOULAGA was born in Cameroon. He is a former professor and director of studies at the Nkol-Bisson Seminary, Yaoundé. Among his forthcoming works is a study of African authenticity and philosophy.

JEAN-MARC ELA was born at Ebolowa, Cameroon. He has published several works on Luther, the black world and the Church, and Jesus Christ and the philosophers. Since 1971 he has been a missionary among the highlanders of the northern Cameroons.

GÉRARD ESCHBACH was born in Strasbourg, France. In 1970 he founded a Centre for Christian Studies and Research at Brazzaville, Congolese Republic, of which he is now director. He has published several works on Christian anthropology, decision processes and Marx and religion.

RENÉ LAURENTIN is a leading French religious journalist, research worker and theologian, among whose many works are recent studies of Theresa of Lisieux and Catholic Pentecostalism.

LUC MOREAU was born at Angers, France. He has been teaching since 1971 at the Higher Institute of Religious Culture at Abidjan, Ivory Coast, and at the Institute of Science and Theology of Religions in Paris.

MGR JOACHIM N'DAYEN is Archbishop of Bangui, Central African Republic (now Empire) and Apostolic Administrator of Bambari.

EFOÉ JULIEN PÉNOUKOU was born in Benin. He was in charge of Catholic broadcasting in Benin where he was a priest at Cotonou. He is completing a thesis in theology at the Catholic Institute in Paris. Among his publications are works on the Gospel and African youth, missions and colonialism, and black intellectuals and changes in mentality.

ANSELME TITIANMA SANON was born at Bobo-Dioulasso in the Upper Volta. He was professor at the Major Seminary of Koumi in the Upper Volta and rector there until nomination as Bishop of Bobo-Dioulasso in 1974. He is the author of many articles.

SIDBE SEMPORÉ, O. P., was born at Ouagadougou, Upper Volta. He has been engaged in pastoral work and biblical teaching at Cotonou, Benin, Abidjan, Ivory Coast, and Ibadan, Nigeria.

MICHAEL SINGLETON is now attached to the Pro Mundi Vita international research centre in Brussels, Belgium. He recently published a dossier on African theology and a bulletin on popular religion, *Let the People Be*. He has researched into various areas of anthropology and spent 1969–72 on and off studying spirit possession in Tanzania.

HAROLD TURNER was born in New Zealand and is a Presbyterian. He has taught in West African universities. He is director of the Project for the Study of New Religious Movements in Primal Societies at Aberdeen University. Among his major works is *African Independent Church* (1967).